Stories of Old Ely and the Lake Country

Mike Hillman

Singing River Publications, Inc.
Ely, MN

Stories of Old Ely and the Lake Country

        Copyright @ 2005 by Mike Hillman
        Second Printing, January 2007

Editor:
        Catherine Holm

Graphic Design:
        CR Graphics, Inc.

Layout:
        IRIS Enterprises

Publisher:
        Singing River Publications, Inc.
        P.O. Box 72
        Ely, MN 55731
        www.singingriverpublications.com

Photography:
        Cover Photo of Mike Hillman by Steve Foss
        Fireplace Photo by "Tom"

The stories in this book are presented to the reader as the author creatively recollects and embellishes them. Much of the information regarding residents mentioned can be corroborated at the Ely Historical Society.

No portion of this book may be reproduced, stored in or introduced into a retrieval system, or transmitted, in any form or by any means -- including photocopying -- without the prior written permission of Singing River Publications, Inc., except in the case of brief quotations embodied in critical articles and reviews. For information, address inquiries to *Singing River Publications, Inc.*

ISBN: 0-9759953-1-6

Printed in Canada

1. Minnesota stories; 2. Ely, Minnesota

To the memory
of
my mom and dad,
Alice and Checker Hillman

Introduction

Laconic phrases came out of Mike Hillman in a natural North Country Poetry. Mike then digressed – all good storytellers digress – to tell me, offhand and by the way, one of the most affecting small-town stories I've ever heard. In Mike Hillman I thought I had stumbled upon the soul of Ely, Minnesota. He is a tenacious and able man of the north. In the spirit of his forebearers, he can do anything he sets his mind to – even if it's something he's never done before. Ely should always belong to people like Iron Mike Hillman, who realize that lakes are the eyes of the earth; people who know enough to thank the Great Spirit for the rice harvest and to tread lightly on the portages.

Charles Kuralt in
Charles Kuralt's America

Table of Contents

Introduction	i
A Bear in the Boat	1
Pounding Nails with a Banana	11
Almost Older Than Time	19
Morses, Hoose, and Other Strange Cases of Hybridization	23
Logging Camp Christmas	27
Stiff as a Board	33
Flowers for Sally	41
Struck By Lightning	45
Mouse Turds and Mike Kelly	49
Prayer Candles	59
The Worst Thing You Ever Did	65
The Last Canoe Trip	75
The Old Shovel	81
The Last Song for Bernice	85
The Mad Miner Or The Tragic Tale of Pick 'Em to Death Pete Peterson	91
The Old Settlers Journal	105
Chief Blackstone's Walk	109
A Rose by Any Other Name	115
The Hanged Man's Tree	125
Anterro F. Tanner	131
Christmas Trees	139
Miss Dahl	143

A Bear in the Boat

Swamp Water Charlie hated bears. He hated bears since the summer when a huge bear, with a head as big as a basketball, came into camp and tore up almost everything Charlie owned. When all was said and done, the only thing left to salvage was a half-eaten bar of Ivory soap. Everything else was torn to shreds.

Swamp Water Charlie declared war on bears that day.

When the topic of bears came up, Charlie would loudly proclaim that the only good bear was a dead bear, and all things were fair in love and war. Every now and then someone would try to defend bears when Swamp Water went on about bruins and what he would like to do to them. The bear defenders pointed out that bears had been here longer that we had. The defenders reminded Charlie that you couldn't blame a bear for being a bear. But nothing anyone could say made the least bit of difference to Charlie.

Swamp Water Charlie came north from Ohio with his partner Donny Beaver in the late 1950s. They were like characters from a Robert W. Service poem; two odd ducks who never seemed to fit in a civilized setting. So, one day, in order to find that place where they wouldn't stand out, they threw everything worth throwing into a battered old Ford and headed north. They read about Ely, Minnesota in an outdoor magazine that talked about living off the land – fish so plentiful they virtually jumped in the boat, deer and moose waiting to be taken, fur-bearing animals almost begging to be turned into fine coats for fancy women. By the time Charlie and Donny finished reading the article, they were hooked. They laid plans and headed north to the Promised Land.

When the two wayfaring strangers reached Bulah Land at the end of a long day-and-a-half ride, they pooled their meager resources and bought all the things needed to start a trap line. But trapping isn't for everyone. In a relatively short period of time, it became apparent that while Donny Beaver had the makings of a fine trapper, Swamp Water Charlie was born for other things. Charlie tried hard to make it as a trapper, but one crisp winter morning when he was snowshoeing the trap line, he came to a trap that had nothing in it but a leg of a bobcat. The cat had chewed its leg off. The sight of that lonely leg sitting there in that trap ended Swamp Water's career as a trapper. Charlie and Donny agreed that when they sold their fur at the end of the season, Donny Beaver would buy out Charlie's share of the enterprise, and Swamp Water would move on to other ventures.

Swamp Water Charlie knocked around after that and found out he wasn't good at a lot of different things. He tried his hand at underground mining only to discover he was claustrophobic. Then he signed on with a local logger. But logging was a tough business, and Charlie came to the conclusion he had an allergy to hard work. He never made it to the end of the season.

If there was one thing Charlie excelled at, it was fishing. Swamp Water Charlie could fish all day long, every day of the year, and it was never enough. So, Charlie decided to make money off the one thing he seemed good at. He would become a professional fishing guide.

It didn't take much to be a professional fishing guide. Back in the 1950s, no rules and regulations governed the wilderness that surrounded Ely, so a guy could pretty much do as he pleased. Swamp Water Charlie had failed at so many things in his life that he wanted to be sure he was going to be successful. The most important thing a fishing guide needs to do is to catch fish, and if there was one lake that offered the best fishing in the entire canoe country it was Basswood Lake. If you couldn't catch fish in Basswood Lake, you couldn't catch fish anywhere. In a land loaded with lakes it was hard not to notice Basswood Lake, a sprawling body of water made up of bays – Pipestone, Jackfish, Merium, Bailey, Ranger, Back, Wind, Hoist, and North Bays – any one of which was big enough to be a lake on its own, and each bay loaded with fish. "Name your poison," the old guys who knew the country would say, "and you'd find it swimming in Basswood Lake." Lake trout, northern pike, bass, and walleye were there in force and ready for the taking.

The first thing Swamp Water Charlie did was to head into the *Ely Miner* newspaper office to talk to Fred Childers, the editor of the paper, in order to get some brochures printed. "What you thinking of calling your business?" asked Fred. "Gonna call it Basswood Guiding Service," answered Charlie. "Good a name as any," replied Fred, and before the week, every outfitting post and fishing shop in town was handing out brochures touting the many advantages of signing on with the Basswood Guiding Service. The first season, Swamp Water Charlie made enough money to keep him drunk and in grub for the entire winter. For the first time in his life Charlie could bask in the reflective glow of his own success. It felt wonderful.

The next season, Charlie had enough money to set up a first-rate fishing camp on Pipestone Bay, a camp hovering on the cutting edge of wilderness camping. He bought two beautiful eight-by-ten white silkaleen wall tents, cots, sleeping bags, cook kit, and a brand spanking new fishing boat complete with a five-horse Evinrude motor. It looked like all the bad luck was behind Charlie and he was bound for success. The people kept coming, the fish kept biting, and the money was rolling in. Swamp Water Charlie was getting to the point in his life that when he stopped at his favorite tavern in between trips he could joke with his friends (who had met him during his formative time) that he was *Mister* Swamp Water Charlie now, complete with a bucket to pee in and a window to throw it out of. But that's when the bear came to call, and everything changed.

On a perfect late June evening, the sand flies, which can make a spring camping trip in Minnesota something of a trial, had passed. One no longer needed any bug dope or a head net until dark came and the mosquitoes came out. But to those who knew the country, mosquitoes were nothing compared to the spring hatch of sand flies. Swamp Water Charlie was bull cooking supper for three anglers from St. Paul who were having the time of their lives limiting out on Basswood Lake. The fishing had been so easy that you almost didn't have to put anything on your hook. They were sitting around camp knocking down Canadian whiskey and basking in the glory of a successful day of fishing. It doesn't get much better than that and everyone in camp was smart enough to know it. Say what you will about sportsmanship, but when you were a fishing guide, it didn't rest in the attempt, it rested with whether you caught fish or not. If the group had been any more successful they would have had to worry about a visit from the game warden. The mosquitoes, which would come out when the sun set, weren't a factor yet and by the time they did come out, the camp would be tucked up in their bunks, protected by the screen netting that was stitched into the tents. It was a wonderful time: a warm summer evening, no bugs, fish cooking on an open fire, good company, and plenty of good whiskey. Then the bear came.

Most people have never experienced a bear in camp, but those that have are almost always taken by surprise that an animal as large as a bear can move so quietly and be right next to you before you know it's there. Swamp Water Charlie had just flipped the fillets in the big black skillet and had reached in the green canvas cook pack to get the salt and pepper shakers. The whole thing took a few seconds, but when Charlie turned back to the fire, there was a bear, with a head like a basketball with ears on it, looking at him, eyeball to eyeball. Swamp Water Charlie's eyes almost popped out of his head as he felt the hot breath on his face. In an instant, walleye fillets headed to heaven as Charlie beat a retreat to the safety of the boat. The fillets fell to earth like manna. They were the first things to be eaten, but certainly not the last.

As soon as the three guys from St. Paul saw the bear, they followed Charlie's lead, piled into the boat, weighed anchor, and headed towards the safety of open water. Swamp Water Charlie's bladder let loose and he felt a course of his own water run down the left leg of his canvas pants. To his credit, Swamp Water caught himself. His three clients were in the process of heading to sea, and Charlie told them to stay close to shore because he was going to fight to regain control of the camp.

Turning back to face that big black bear was one of the bravest things Charlie ever did. He had always thought about bringing a gun with him, but the only thing close to a weapon in camp was the double-bit axe to split firewood. He pulled it from the splitting stump and headed back to do battle. In the light of the setting sun he looked like a malnourished character from a Frank Frazetta sketch.

A black bear on all fours doesn't look all that impressive, and when Swamp Water Charlie made his way back to camp, axe in hand, with bad intentions in his heart, he started to shout and curse that big black bear. Bruno had finished the fish and spuds and was tearing at the food pack. Swamp Water Charlie knew how much that green canvas packsack cost, and he summoned up all that was in him and charged at the bear. He remembered his grandmother telling him that one of his great uncles served with Bobby Lee in some of the hottest battles of the Civil War. Charlie let out with the best version of the rebel yell that he could in order to put the fear of God into that bear. But this was a northern bear that didn't cotton to rebels, and when he heard Swamp Water Charlie coming at him like something out of the Stonewall Brigade, the bear stood up on his hind legs and stopped Charlie dead in his tracks.

If a black bear doesn't look like much on all fours, all that changes when it stands on its back legs, arches its back, and bares its teeth. Standing vertical changes everything. When a black bear is threatened, even by something as feeble as Swamp Water Charlie, it clacks its back teeth together in an impressive snapping sound designed to give second thoughts to anyone the bear perceives as a threat. That bear, which looked to be about four foot tall, stood up, clacking its teeth, now about eight foot tall or better. All the intentions Charlie had about doing bad things to that bear withered up and died in Charlie's heart. Swamp Water Charlie dropped the axe, turned away from the bear, and headed back to the safety of the water. It was a long night sitting in the boat.

Things weren't so bad at first. One of the guys from St. Paul had the foresight, as he beat a retreat toward the boat, to grab a bottle of whiskey, which lasted to sunset. Then the mosquitoes came out. The bug dope was still in camp. It seemed as if the mosquitoes applauded the voracious bruin that busily devoured anything remotely edible.

It was amazing to see how much damage one bear could do and even more amazing to see how much that bear could eat. Just when Swamp Water Charlie thought things couldn't be worse, a thunderstorm rolled through about the time things were starting to gray up. In the dim light of a damp and chill morning, the men sat like four drowned rats as that pumpkin-headed bear waddled off into the woods with a soft grunting *ugh, ugh, ugh* that to the Ojibway, sounded like *muck-wa*. Swamp Water Charlie would always remember that sound of pure contentment.

When the group hit the shore and made a search of what was left of camp, the only thing worth saving was a half-eaten bar of soap. Everything else was smashed, shredded, or eaten. Swamp Water declared war on bears. He vowed that as soon as he made enough money to put together another cache, he was going to buy himself the biggest gun in town, and then them damn bears had best watch out.

Later that summer, Charlie was heading up to camp with a boatload of provisions for two gangsters from Chicago. The gangsters had done a job in Detroit and were cooling off and keeping out of trouble by catching monster pike on Jackfish Bay. About the time Charlie was nearing his destination, what should he spy just ahead of him but a bear with a head that looked like a basketball with ears, swimming towards Swamp

Water Charlie's camp. Charlie stood up in the back of the boat like Captain Ahab in *Moby Dick*. He looked up to heaven, shook a raised fist, and swore an oath that this incarnation of evil, that had done him so much harm, would never reach the shore.

A five-horse Evinrude motor on a fourteen-foot boat is nothing anyone is going to water-ski behind, and for a while it seemed a matter of debate to the two men sitting in camp just which was the faster – the boat or the bear. Slowly it became apparent that Swamp Water Charlie was putt-putting at a faster rate and had drawn even with the bear. In a move filled with malice and designed to drive that bothersome bruin beneath the waves, Charlie cut the boat right at the bear, but he missed. At the last moment the bear figured if someone was trying to run you over with a boat, the smart thing to do would be to head the other way, which is exactly what the bear did. All Charlie would have had to do was to let that bear do exactly what it intended, which was to get to camp and do the same thing to Swamp Water Charlie that the bear had done earlier in the summer. Those two gangsters, who waited patiently for provisions that weren't meant to be shared with no damn bear, were packing enough heat to take care of every bear in the canoe country. The gangsters were, in fact, debating who was going to have the honor of ending the bear's career and starting its new existence as a rug in Chicago.

But at that moment Swamp Water Charlie was as mad as Ahab chasing the white whale. The two men stood on shore, brandishing pistols in one hand and making Italian gestures with the other, and yelling for Charlie to head Bruno back their way. Charlie turned, and with a glazed, biblical, righter-than-god look, told them this bear was his and no one could come between a man and his bear. Each time that bear would almost reach the shore, the pygmy Pequod would chase it back toward deeper water. At each moment of truth, the skipper would laugh and swear oaths to dark gods to let him have his pound of flesh. All the bear understood was that if it didn't do something soon it was going to drown. It wasn't thought that saved that bear, it was instinct. In a last gasp of life force, that tired bear surged up out of the water and grabbed hold of the side of the boat.

Swamp Water Charlie watched in horror as the nearly exhausted bear, with nothing left to fear, climbed cumbersomely aboard. Charlie looked for something to repel the boarder, but the ores, which could have done the job, were sitting below the supplies. All the besieged captain could do was shout at the bear and cry for help from the two avenging angels standing on the shore. The boat headed away from camp, and even men who used guns to make a living didn't want to chance shooting the one man who knew the way home. They pulled up their guns and waited for a safe chance to bag the bear.

In an effort to regain control of his small craft, Charlie gulped down the last of the flask he had been sipping on as he headed back to camp, and hurled the container at the bear, which was establishing a secure beachhead in the bow of the boat. In a reflex action older than time, when the errant bottle passed by its head, the bear clacked his teeth in an effort to put fear into the heart of its enemy. In the mind of Swamp Water Charlie, that clacking of back teeth was as terrifying as the sound of the clock in the belly of Captain Hook's alligator. Swamp Water Charlie took the coward's way out of the situation and chose not to go down with the ship. He jumped out of the back of the boat. The two gangsters fired a few shots just as the boat disappeared around the point heading north.

Uno and Urho Koski were fishing on the other side of the point and drinking some home-brewed liquor, known locally as Kick-A-Poo Joy Juice. The bear passed them as it headed toward Canada. The first thing they thought of was taking the temperance pledge. Urho turned to Uno and asked him what in the hell had he put into this batch of moonshine. All Urho could say was, "Nothing special." They were both thankful that Urho had brought a camera along that was intended to capture images of trophy fish. On this day and for years to come they were glad that whenever they told the story of the bear in a boat, they were able to take out the grainy black and white pictures bearing witness to what they saw.

Nobody exactly knows what happened to Swamp Water Charlie. Some say he hopped a train and headed home to Ohio. Others say he started swimming north in hot pursuit of that damned pumpkin-headed bear in order to get back his boat and all his stuff. The last thing anyone saw of the bear was when he stopped to buy gas at Zup's Fishing Camp at Curtain Falls, and inquired about the abundance of the blueberry and hazel nut crops. Neither boat nor bear has been seen since.

Pounding Nails with a Banana

No one will ever forget the winter of 1995-96 if they lived in Northern Minnesota. They might not remember exactly what year it was; people's minds are like that. I can't remember the year of the big All Saints Night blizzard. All I remember is standing a block from my house with my son and daughter, feeling the wind come up, and watching the snow flying on the horizontal. I turned to Ren and Stimpy and told them it was time to go home. The next morning I woke up with over two feet of snow on the ground. It's something I will never forget. The trouble is I can't ever remember which year it was. That's the same way it is with Ground Hog's Day back in ninety-something, when it was so cold you could pound nails with a banana.

1995 was the first year I managed the local radio for Charles Kuralt. He had come to Ely the summer of 1993 to refresh his memory of one of his favorite American places. Charles had recently finished his tenure with CBS television, and he said goodbye to us on Sunday Morning. It didn't seem all that long since I watched him say, "Farewell my friends, farewell and hale, I'm bound to seek the Holy Grail. Remember please when I am gone, 'twas aspiration drove me on. Toodley woodely woodely woo, all I want is to stay with you, but here I go, goodbye." He wanted to call the book *My Favorite Year,* but in the end they agreed on the name *Charles Kuralt's America.*

I asked Kuralt once how he had survived so long in a place like CBS News, with all the big and hungry fish who swam in its waters, and Charles answered my question by telling me he survived by going on the road. During the course of his travels he got to visit many different places and one of them happened to be Ely, Minnesota. Charles had come to visit Dorothy Molter on the Isle of the Pines on Knife Lake. He fell in love with the place, and according to Charles Kuralt, there was no finer place to be than Ely during the month of July. He came back twenty years later to pay a visit, and to figure out just why he liked the place so much. Charles was staying in a cabin on Moose Lake, and that's how we got to meet. It was a Sunday morning, and Charles tried to figure out how to make the television work, but he couldn't figure it out, so he turned to the next best thing – the radio. When he turned it on he found out that the only station he could get was the local radio station, and that's when he heard my radio show.

  I had just come back from an eleven-day trip through the Boundary Waters; just about the best trip I ever had. We had traveled over two hundred miles by canoe, and seen wonderful country. On the radio show, I talked about some of the special places my partner and I had seen during the trip, and played some special music in honor of the occasion. At the end of the show the phone rang and a sonorous voice told me that it had been a long time since he had enjoyed a radio program as much as he enjoyed mine. He asked if I would be willing to visit with him. We met a couple days later over coffee and homemade blueberry pie, and I told him everything I knew about the place. We spent two afternoons visiting with each other, and I got to have my picture taken with him, but I truly never thought that we would see each other again.

  A few weeks later I was laid off from the station, and my wife Julie wrote Charles a letter to tell him that I was no longer working at the station. A few days later, a letter arrived from Charles. He was genuinely saddened to hear that the local station had lost its best programmer. Then he made an offer to buy the station if I agreed to manage it, and when the station went bankrupt later that year, it worked out that Charles made the highest bid, and I became the Manager of what we called The

End of the Road Radio.

When we started our partnership I asked him what he expected of me, and the first thing he said was that he didn't expect me to make any money, but he was worried that I might lose too much. He told me that all he wanted was the best radio station possible, and that's what we set out to do. I asked Charles if he had known Edward R. Morrow. His eyes lit up, and he told me that he was in the room when Morrow lost control of CBS News. Charles told me that Morrow looked up and told everyone in the room, "When a business like ours loses its sense of place and contact with its people, it is nothing but a soul-less box of wires." Morrow walked out of the room. I told Charles that whatever might happen, we would never end up being a soul-less box of wires. He was about the best person I ever worked for.

We didn't know it when we started that summer, when the whole country seemed to be ablaze, and the sun turned into a blood-red disk in a smoky sky, that the coming winter would have its own surprises. The snow came in mid November, and it kept coming and coming, from then until the end of December. Things cleared up in January, and the bottom fell out from the thermometer. From New Year to the end of the month the temperature never got close to above freezing. First we passed the forty-below mark, which is darn cold even in Minnesota. That was a warm up for what was to come. In the third week of the month, we broke the fifty-below mark, and it stayed that way. Day after day it was fifty below or better at the start of the day, and we would be lucky to get to forty below for the day's high temperature. The only thing that saved the water and sewer lines was the snow on the ground.

On the first day of February the official temperature in Embarrass was fifty-eight degrees below zero. Down in Tower it was fifty-nine below, and they said it was going to be colder in the morning. It's hard for people to believe that any place that depended on tourism would want anyone to know that it was that cold, but by that time we were making the national news. Chances were good that we would break the all-time record for cold since they had been keeping track of such things. Our station had a fellow ready to head down to Embarrass and sleep out in one of the snow houses they had built near the weather station, but we had no one going to Tower. That's where I wanted to be. I had kept track of the two area cold spots and the thing I noticed was that more often than not, the Kugler Township station near Tower was usually the colder of the two. I had a chance to make history.

Sixty below zero is nothing to take lightly. I had spent a month camping out in a tent when we were moving some buildings on Snowbank Lake, and I did see some nights when it got down to the mid-forties. I remembered how cold that was, and I wanted to make sure I had the equipment to handle temperatures that cold. I went down to the Northwoods Company to talk to my friend Steve Piragis, and I asked him if he had a sleeping bag that would handle sixty below. Steve asked me why I wanted to know, and I told him that I was going to take my tent down to Tower and sleep out at Kathy Hoppa's weather station. He smiled and told me that there wasn't a single bag that would handle cold like that, so I would have to double bag it. Steve picked out two of his best sleeping bags, and a special hood to wear over my head so my nose and ears wouldn't freeze. I asked Steve if he was sure that I would wake up with a full contingent of fingers and toes. Steve looked at me and said with all the press coverage this was generating, the last thing he wanted was for the media to find me frozen in his sleeping bags. I thanked him and headed toward Tower.

Three television stations watched me struggle to put up my tent. Everything tightens up in the cold, and the fabric of my tent was so puckered that I had all I could do to get the end of the tent poles into the proper grommet. When I finished the struggle I could see freeze burns on my hands from the metal poles. Fortune Bay Resort and Casino provided me with a fine surf and turf dinner, but when I put the first piece of steak into my mouth, the fork froze to my lips, and I had to blow on it, so it wouldn't rip the skin from my lips. After dinner everyone left and I settled down for the night.

The only heat I had was a candle, more for the light than anything else. I listened to the radio until the batteries froze and tried to do some reading, but found it difficult with mittens on, so I gave up. I had a few pulls on a bottle of cinnamon schnapps, and then I lay there thinking of Robert W. Service poems, of those hard luck men who wintered up in the Yukon. I remember thinking I was the fourth generation of my family to call this place home, but none of them had ever seen it this cold, and with any luck I would see history made in the morning. The last thing I remember is hearing the wolves howling down in the swamp that surrounded the hill where I camped next to the weather station. It was a sad and lonely sound. I hunkered down in the comforting warmth of my sleeping bags, feeling grateful I wasn't a wolf.

In the morning the press started to gather before dawn to see history made. A friend who ran a local bed and breakfast brought me a home-built breakfast to start my day. We were all somewhat disappointed when we saw the temperature was sitting at fifty-eight below, but Kathy Hoppa told us not to worry, because it would get colder after sun up. When the sun rose and shone on the pines in Kathy's front yard, it caused them to heat up from convection. When the hot air started to rise it pulled the colder air up from the swamp, so there was nothing to do but wait for the sun. We were surprised when word came from Embarrass that they wouldn't be able to record a temperature on this Ground Hog Day morning. A news team had pointed their camera at the thermometer in Roland Fowler's weather station, and the heat from the light on the camera shattered Roland's thermometer. It was up to Tower.

About a half hour after sunrise the thermometer dropped to fifty-nine below, and a cheer went up from the press corps. Kathy was upset when someone from Embarrass wondered why it could get colder when the sun came up, and there was some implication in the question that perhaps something funny was up in Tower. What could you do, I wondered, to make it colder when you're already below the temperature of dry ice?

A car pulled into the yard, and a fellow came out carrying a short two-by-four, some nails, and a bunch of bananas. He introduced himself, told everyone that one of his goals in life was to have his picture taken in every city in Minnesota, and that he thought today would be a good day to have a picture done in Tower. He looked at us and said that his grandfather told him when it got down past fifty below, you could pound nails with bananas.

He set the board on the ground, took a nail in his left hand, grabbed one of the frozen bananas in his right, and proceeded to drive a nail into the wood with a piece of tropical fruit that never dreamed of being in such a situation. I told him to pass me the board, and when I tried to pull out the nail with my hand, I found I couldn't do it.

"Give me a nail and a fresh banana," I said. For the first and – I hope – the last time in my life, I pounded a nail with a banana. I thought of hundreds of winter construction workers tossing their hammers for bananas, then eating their tropical hammers for lunch.

We looked up as Kathy came out of the house and made her way over to the white box. The thermometer would tell us whether or not history was going to be made this Ground Hog Day morning. She opened the door, and with a dozen or so people looking over her shoulder, Kathy told us that the official temperature was now sixty below.

History had been made. Later on the temperature would drop another two degrees. When you stood where the hill spilled down into the swamp, you could actually feel the cold moving up the hill, as the sun heated the pines. It was the best example of convection I have ever seen. When we found that Kathy had a spare thermometer, Marshall Helmberger, the editor of the local paper, asked if we could take the spare down to the bottom of the swamp, and Kathy said fine. We walked down into the valley of cold and stood there for several minutes before I watched the blood retreat from Marshall's nose.

"Marshall," I said, "I don't know how cold it is, but your nose just froze, and we've got to get you inside." Without a word he handed me the thermometer as he walked up the hill.

The thermometer read seventy-two degrees below zero. I followed Marshall up the hill to the warmth of Kathy Hoppa's kitchen.

Later that same day I rode into Ely and found people out on the streets throwing boiling pans of water up in the air, watching it turn to steam in the cold air. I got back at the radio station and found a message on my desk from Charles Kuralt, asking me to give him a call. I picked up the phone. In a few seconds my friend's voice greeted me.

"So you didn't freeze to death?" he asked.

"Not too badly," I answered.

Then Charles asked, "So tell me, just how cold was it in Tower, Minnesota?"

I thought for a moment, and I saw the fellow pounding the nail with the banana. "Charles, it was so cold in Tower this morning, that you could pound nails with a banana."

"That's great," Charles responded, "Do you mind if I pass that down the line?" I told him that he was welcome to it, and then I went home to take care of my ears, which had suffered the same fate as Marshall's nose. The last thing I remember from the day is hearing David Brinkley say on the nightly news, "And just how cold was it in Tower, Minnesota this morning? It was cold enough that you could pound nails with a banana. Keep warm, and goodnight from ABC News."

The next morning, Charles called. What I had given him had grown into a minor media classic. I asked what he meant, and he told me that the banana line had been used on every major news network. He thought I was being figurative, but I told him the truth. I can still hear him say, with an incredulous voice. "Do you mean to tell me that someone really did pound nails with a banana?"

"That's right Charles. I watched him do it, and then I pounded one in myself."

There was a short pause. "That's incredible. Do you know it was colder in Tower yesterday than it was at either the North or South Poles? I've been to the North Pole," he said, "I was in the coldest place on earth once, and I had to travel hundreds of miles to do it. You were too, and all you had to do was to drive twenty miles and pitch your tent in Kathy Hoppa's yard. Life is strange sometimes. But be that as it may, it was still a fine thing. Cold enough to pound nails with a banana. What a great line."

Almost Older Than Time

It had been a number of years since I had seen the old rock chimney, and I was glad to see it still standing. The chimney was the last thing left from what had been Hibbard's Lodge. Later on, when I knew the place, it had been sold a couple of times, and renamed Tanglewood Trail Lodge. I ran a canoe base just down the shore when I attended college. I would go to the resort at the end of the day to visit with Tanglewood Ted, and have a bite to eat. The main lodge hadn't burnt yet, and it was fun to sit and visit with the different people who came to vacation on Moose Lake. Some of them had been coming for years, and it was always interesting meeting old and new friends.

Ted was married when he first started running the resort, but after a couple of years his wife couldn't handle resort life, and went back home. After that Ted ran things by himself. I'd like to think that Ted had some good years running what had been a dream of his. But I think by the end of things, the dream may have turned into a nightmare. The lodge burnt down in the late 1970s and from then on, until he took sick, Ted ran the operation from one of the bigger cabins that had been built around that old rock chimney.

Sometime in the 1980s Ted fought a losing battle with cancer, and the resort sat empty. I heard some talk that there was a dispute between Ted's brother and Ted's estranged wife. By the time the dust had settled, the resort had pretty well fallen apart, and the government ended up buying the place.

I visited Tanglewood a few years after Ted died, and it was one of the saddest things I ever saw. A place that had once been filled with people was now deserted. I remember walking into Ted's cabin, and on the floor was the old red baseball cap he always wore. It's funny in a way how a simple thing like someone's hat can reach out and touch you but that old red hat, lying on the floor, touched me. It bothered me that after his death, nobody had gone through his things. People had busted into the cabin, took what they wanted, and trashed the place. Flour had been dumped on the floor, and Ted's clothes and papers were scattered all over. I picked up the best I could, and I was so upset I called his daughter and told her that someone should come and take a look to see if they might not want to claim some of the letters.

The neighbors across the small bay, that separated the resort from their homes on the south shore, let it be known they didn't like the idea of a resort opening up again. The government decided to tear the resort down. A few years after they tore it down I was out visiting my old canoe base, and I decided to pay a visit to see what was left of Tanglewood Lodge. Nobody had walked the old path for years, but I was surprised to see that other than a few trees blocking the way, the path was still there and quite visible. I walked with mixed feelings. Like most people, I hate when things change, and part of me wished I was walking over to pick up a sandwich, and to listen to Ted tell people why the fish weren't biting. Ted had hundreds of different reasons why they weren't biting, but not one suggestion for getting them to bite. But that was something from another time.

After looking around I realized there wasn't much left to remind people of what had stood on the point. Other than a few rock foundations, the only thing left standing was the old stone fireplace. I remember standing in front of the chimney when the sun came out from behind the clouds, and the rocks in the fireplace came alive with the sun. I had never seen it in the sunshine before, and it was truly a thing of beauty. The old chimney had been built sometime in the 1930s by none other than John Y. Brown, better known to history as Rock A Day Brown. Anyone who had Rock A Day Brown work for them would agonize over the amount of time he took to put together a fireplace, which seemed to proceed at a pace of about a stone a day. He selected his rocks with the greatest of care, but when he finished the job, anyone who looked at Rock A Day Brown's work had to admit it was a work of art.

No two Rock A Day Brown's fireplaces were alike. I had been lucky enough to see a half dozen or so of his very special chimneys, but I think of those, the one he built for Hibbard's Lodge was the best. He used every different kind of rock that was found in this country, and that old chimney was the perfect mix of geology. Pink and white granite, mixed in with greenstone and iron, set next to jasper and quartz, which was interspersed with gabro and pyrite. Standing in front of that chimney was like looking at a poem written in stone. Some of the rock had once lain on the floor of ancient seas, but when the granite came up from deep in the earth, the rock had been folded and tipped on end. Rock that once lay horizontal was now stacked vertical, and even that was represented in Brown's chimney. I remember standing in front of that lonely chimney and thinking, *they don't make them like that any more.* I believe that's why they didn't tear it down when the rest of the resort went back to nature. In a world where everything needs to be done quickly, it was a comfort to know that some things, such as Rock A Day Brown's rock chimney, are just too beautiful to tear down.

According to geologists, the granite came up around two point three billion years, and that's the furthest they can date things, because any rock that was here before the granite had its clock reset by millions of years of heat and pressure. We know the greenstone and iron were here first, but we just can't date it. Some of the rocks used in the old chimney were older than time. It's hard to think about just how long ago that was, and I started to think if you measured time in feet, right now my life's journey would be just over five feet. If you went back to when the first people were making tools on Knife Lake twelve thousand years ago, it would be a distance of just over two miles. To get back to the time the rock was made and travel those two thousand three hundred million years, the distance would be right around 435,606 miles, and that's a long way to travel.

I think the old chimney will stand long after I am gone, but I can see a day on down the line when the mortar that holds the rocks in place will give up its battle with time, and collapse. One day, years and years from now, someone might be walking along the shore of Moose Lake and come upon a pile of rocks, and wonder how they got there. They won't know of me, or Tanglewood Ted, or Rock a Day Brown, but until that time, let the old chimney stand as a monument to what has gone before, and to all the different people who once called the point home. But let it also stand as a reminder that nothing is older than time.

Morses, Hoose, and Other Strange Cases of Hybridization

Ely – June 27th, 2004. In a recently released study, Dr. I. M. Blinder of the University of Saskatoon announced an official sighting of a hoose less than twenty miles northwest of Ely. This documented sighting of the legendary animal, a supposed cross between a horse and a moose, is the first verified sighting since 1933 when the state declared both the hoose, and its close cousin, the morse, on the list of endangered species.

Dr. Blinder has been studying these legendary animals since the official study began in 1984, as part of a jointly funded venture between the University of Saskatoon, Minnesota DNR, and Vermilion Community College. In a statement released earlier this week, Dr. Blinder calls this sighting one of the true highlights of his life, and the culmination of a lifetime of dedication and study of these rare hybrids.

Born in rural northeastern Minnesota, Dr. Blinder became interested in these animals when he was a boy hanging out at Arvo's Tavern. Old lumberjacks would tell stories of seeing morses and hoose wandering around the deep woods of northern Minnesota. According to the legend, the origin of the hybrids dates back to the end of the nineteenth century when logging was beginning its halcyon days. There were dozens of logging camps, and hundreds of men working in the woods for any number of different companies. Most of the teamster work was done by horses, and according to Dr. Blinder there were dozens of these tote teams scattered across hundreds of miles of what would soon be logged off forest.

In the fall of 1899, many forest fires that raged across the state threatened the well-being of the animals. In an effort to save as many of the animals as possible, the logging camps released their horses. It was the only way the horses had a chance of surviving the holocaust. The loggers hoped the animals would make their way to water, or find some other way to avoid the fires.

When the flames were extinguished by the first snows of winter, and the loggers made their way back into the forests, the first thoughts were about locating the missing horses. Dr. Blinder told the press that according to the records kept by logging clerks, many of the horses had indeed survived the fires, but a fair number of them could not be accounted for. It was assumed the missing animals had either died in the fires, or had become the victim of perdition by wolves and other predators.

The first sighting of the hybrid animal was made in 1905 by Tauno Lampi, who later founded the Knights of Temperance Society. According to Lampi's report to the editor of the *Ely Miner* newspaper, Lampi was working on his back forty when he saw this animal that was a cross between a moose and a horse, but not quite either. When queried about the looks of the animal, Lampi stated that it mostly had the head and body of a horse, but the legs of a moose. They decided to refer to the animal as a morse. In an interesting side note, the Town of Morse, which surrounds the City of Ely, takes its name from this legendary animal.

Shortly after the start of 1906, Elmer Larson, a teamster for the St. Croix Company, was hauling out a load of logs when a strange looking animal crossed in front of his team. According to Larson, a deacon in the Lutheran Church, the animal had the head of horse, supporting a trophy rack of antlers. It had a body about half way between either animal. The legs were mostly moose, the logger stated, but three of them had white socks, and there was a white star-shaped blaze on the animal's face. When asked about what was on the animal's south end, Larson stated that the white tail would have made a fine addition to any horse. Larson dubbed the animal a hoose. When asked if the animal made any sort of sound, the sober-faced teamster answered that when the hoose saw the tote team, it made a bleating sort of whinny, and crashed off into the forest.

According to I. M. Blinder, the next thirty years were filled with sightings of these reclusive animals. The sightings generated much discussion, and conclusions were reached by the best scientists of the time. The animals in all probability were a crossbreed that stemmed back to the fall of 1899 when horses were released into the forest to escape death by fire. Dr. Blinder sighted an interesting report compiled in 1910 by Professor Wilber Ostenwald, a science teacher at Bemidji State Teachers College. According to the extensive report there is little doubt that horses and moose had successfully mated. Professor Ostenwald's only major question was whether morses and hoose were the same, or different, sub-species of hybrids. In the same report, the professor also stated that other reports about the horses having bred with woodland caribou, named the upland horseybou, were probably false.

Dr. Blinder stated that this is one of the important matters still up for debate. One of the study's goals is to collect samples of both animals' DNA in order to settle the matter once and for all. Dr. Blinder has even devised a humane live trap specially designed to accomplish the capture of either animal in a humane and compassionate way. Dealing with these animals can be life threatening, and Dr. Blinder mentioned the many reports from people who ran into them in the autumn. Almost every report stated that there was no fiercer animal in the northern forest than a bull hoose in rut.

One thing complicated the study. According to a few old loggers, the meat of the hoose and morse was exceptionally delicious, and because it wasn't a native species, there were no rules governing its harvest. Hoose and morse were also coveted as a trophy mount, but sad to say, none of the mounts are known to exist today. So much hunting pressure was placed on these animals that they retreated to the deep parts of the forest, and were rarely seen. The state finally put both the hoose and the morse on the list of endangered species, along with the agropelter and wampus cat in the summer of 1933.

But in spite of the efforts at preservation, it was feared the animal might have been hunted to extinction until a group of mushroom pickers from San Francisco, California, reported sighting one of the animals in 1972. The sighting led to the current study.

When asked how the study was being funded, Dr. Blinder informed us that a bill sponsored by Senator Hiram Boondoggle of New Jersey was pending on the floor of the Senate. Wanting to demonstrate his concern for preservation and the advancement of science, Senator Boondoggle included funding for the further study of the morse and hoose as part of a package involving highway funding and a power plant for his home state. The Blinder Bill has been called one of the most shortsighted and blindest bills ever seen in the Senate. Nonetheless we wish the good doctor well in his quest to be the first man to tackle the issue of whether the hoose and morse are one or two species.

Harvey Chandler

Logging Camp Christmas

Dear Mamma and Papa,

I know that I haven't written as much as I should, but I wanted to be sure to wish you a Merry Christmas and Happy New Year. I have been very busy since the first part of October working as a swamper and conman for the Knox Lumber Company. Those are lumberjack terms for any man who works on the logging roads that go deep into the woods, so the axe men and sawyers can cut down the large pines that will go to the mills next spring. Most of the work in the camp starts after things have been cold enough to freeze in the swamps, but because I worked hard last year, I was hired for the crew of swampers who start earlier than the other men. This fall we cut the roads to the pinery that we are now harvesting.

I don't want you to think that because what I do is called a conman that it is something bad. Now that the cold weather has arrived, I drive through the cuttings maintaining the ice roads that the teamsters use to get the logs out of the woods. I think the name comes from the fact that I help construct the roads. All day long I drive a team of heavy horses up and down the roads in the water wagon. As we go down the road, a slow stream of water drips down from the water tank, in order to smooth out the roads that get pretty roughed up with all the logs that are hauled on them. In the real cold weather I have a small stove on the water wagon just below the tank to keep things from freezing solid.

This Christmas finds me in an eighty-man logging camp

about six miles from a small town in northern Minnesota named Ely. America is a huge country and Minnesota is much different and better for me than New York City. I like this part of America because it reminds me of home.

There is plenty of work and opportunity here. This year they are paying me thirty dollars a month with room and board thrown in to boot, which is more money than I thought I would see in my life. Some of the men who worked hard and learned the trade are making fifty dollars a month, and I don't see why that couldn't be me in a while. I was listening to some men talking the other night and they were saying that if a man really wanted to have steady work and make big money, he needed to work in one of the iron mines. I don't doubt the miners make good money, but from what I have heard about the conditions those men work under, I don't know if I would care for such a life. I prefer my candle on the bed stand and not on my hat.

Right now it's getting late in the afternoon and I'm sitting at the eating table in the cook shack. Normally, Mr. Anderson, the Butter and Egg Man, would never let me in the cook shack to write a letter. But being as how it is Christmas, and there is no work today except for the cooks who are rattling away in the kitchen, and Mr. Anderson is in an exceptionally good mood, he has been kind enough to let me use his table to write this letter. Sitting here smelling the fresh baked bread and cookies reminds me of home. Mr. Anderson is a first rate belly robber, and he and the other cooks will do their best in the kitchen today, but his dinner won't be near as good as one of yours, Mamma. He can't afford to put the love in them that you did and I think today that love was always your secret ingredient.

Last night many of the men headed to town to enjoy Christmas in the saloons and bawdy houses, but most of the God-fearing men spent Christmas here in camp where many lonely letters have been penned to faraway homes. Last night our boss, Moonlight Johnson, read from the bible, and Eino Maki played some old Christmas hymns on the fiddle. We are sure lucky to have Eino in our camp, for his beautiful fiddle music helps us pass the time in the evenings.

The men call Mr. Johnson Moonlight on account of him keeping us out in the woods working late on clear nights. Mr. Johnson is one of the big bulls of the woods who has a reputation to maintain, so on winter nights when the moon is bright he likes to keep us out working long after the sun has gone to bed. He's one of those hard-driving men who I don't mind working for, because he is fair in his dealings with the men, and he runs a good camp.

I know you worry about me, but I want you to know they treat me pretty good here, and they feed me like a king. This morning we woke up at five with Mr. Anderson banging on his big skillet and yelling, "Everybody out, it's Christmas in the swamps." Today we enjoyed our usual big breakfast with the only difference being that we were allowed to talk at the table. Mr. Anderson likes to say that talking takes time away from eating, and at a logging camp, time is money. With that many men eating on tin plates and drinking tea from tin cups it sounds like a regular symphony in tin, making talking hard in the first place.

Today we woke up to bacon, fried potatoes, pancakes, biscuits, oatmeal, fresh donuts, and last night's pregnant woman, or as most people know it, apple pie. If today was a regular day we'd be out in the woods working, and about 11:30 everyone's belly would start to rumble. We'd all be waiting to hear one of the cookies blow the gabriel, or dinner horn, calling us to lunch. Last year we were close enough to camp to come in for dinner, but this year they loaded dinner into a small sled with a swinging cover that we use as a table. The sled and table are called the swingdingle, and it's filled to the brim with grub, because lunch is the big meal of the day. Today I'm still stuffed by a camp dinner of roast pork, rutabagas, bean hole beans, dried fruit, raisin pie, cookies, donuts, and coffee. Tonight we will sit down to a supper of soup, biscuits, johnny cake, beef stew, cold meat, potatoes, beans, and a special Christmas cake Mr. Anderson is baking in honor of the day. But none of it reaches those Christmas dinners that Mamma used to make.

Tonight we'll welcome Father Buh to our camp for a special Christmas service. He's one of those truly good men who can put into practice what he preaches. Mr. Johnson says Father Buh can read and write fifteen different languages and converse in ten others, including Ojibway, the language of the Indian people here. That makes him one of the greatest living linguists in the state of Minnesota, and maybe America. He gave mass in his home church in Tower this morning, then put on his snowshoes and made the rounds of the logging camps where God's work needs doing. He'll read to us from the Bible, then offer his healing services to any poor jack who needs a little free medical advice. Father Buh knows quite a lot about the healing plants around here, and his remedies are highly regarded.

Last Christmas some of the axe men asked the Father if he would bless their axes, and of course he obliged them. Lumberjacks are a suspicious lot, who never sharpen axes on Sunday because it brings bad luck. And some won't stay in a bunkhouse that has any popple logs in it because that's the wood they used in Christ's Cross. And don't ask them to start any new projects on a Friday.

If you saw how many clothes I wear everyday you wouldn't worry about me being cold. I wear two pairs of two-piece red wool underwear – I like them much better than a union suit. On top of that I wear either one or two wool shirts depending on how cold it is, heavy wool stag pants, a mackinaw jacket, wool cap, two pairs of mitts, two pairs of socks, and pack boots. I think the only thing I have to worry about is breaking through the ice on one of the lakes from all that heavy clothing.

Every night when we come in, we hang our clothes on the balsam rack above the pot-bellied stove that heats the bunkhouse. Then they're dried out by morning when we get up for another day's work. With almost two hundred socks drying, you can imagine how things smell in the bunkhouse.

Well, the shanty boys are starting to set the table for tonight's Christmas supper, so it's time for me to pack up my pencil and paper and put your Christmas letter in an envelope along with a little money, then put it into the camp's mailbag. Know that I love and miss you all. I don't know when I will see you again. I like America pretty well and, like anything else, the more time you spend doing something the more you get used to it. All my love and blessings. Merry Christmas and Happy New Year from your son in America.

    Love, John

Stiff as a Board

The only thing my father was passionate about was fishing. In his heyday Dad spent most of his weekends from ice-out to freeze-up chasing walleye and trout on the Canadian side of the canoe country. As he grew older Dad stayed closer to home, and did most of his fishing from shore. Dad had arrived at the point in his fishing life when he was past the point of buying live bait when the fishing world was liquid, and would spend hours casting various types of wooden minnows. They worked as well as the real thing, and it was a rare occasion when he didn't come home with a meal of fish.

Anyone who knows Northern Minnesota will tell you that the winters are long and cold. There are some who feel there are really only three seasons up north; just before winter, winter, and just after winter. From the end of November and sometimes even to the end of March, the lakes are frozen solid enough that you can drive cars and trucks on them. I ran the canoe base on Moose Lake, and people from down south had a hard time believing that the ice would ever be that thick. One winter I drove my car out on the ice in front of the canoe base and took a picture of it, so people could see I was telling the truth, at least regarding the thickness of the ice.

Dad never liked being cold, so in order to keep fishing in the winter, he built himself a portable canvas ice shelter, long before they came into fashion. It was basically square in shape, narrow at the top and flaring out at the bottom, and allowed plenty of room for two holes. One Christmas, Mother bought him a fine goose down sleeping bag. The bag allowed him to spend time sleeping in his shelter on those trips he made with his friends Johnny and Joe. Johnny bought one of the first snowmobiles in town and in a true act of faith, the three of them would head into the frozen wilderness.

The machine was a huge and heavy beast that lumbered across the frozen lakes like a tired old metal horse. Once on a slow fishing day, I asked Johnny if I could take it for a ride around the lake. Johnny looked at me and said that the Polaris wasn't meant for joy riding, it was meant for getting to and from fishing spots. I can still see them standing there on a cold winter morning, clad in air force flight suits, and cumbersome white felt boots. They were called bunny boots, because they would keep your feet as warm as a bunny, and they were the best cold weather boots available at the time. The only problem was when the gray Polaris would bog down in a pocket of slush, the men had to get off the machine and push until they found better going. The major fault with felt boots was that they weren't made for water. On more than one occasion, Dad would come back with a pair of frozen boots that looked for all the world like elephant feet. Mother would spread towels on the kitchen floor near the sink until the boots would thaw enough to get them off.

By the time my father retired, most of his big adventures on the Canada side were done, and he spent most of his winters down on the ice in front of Joe Buchner's hanger on Shagawa Lake. Father had done Joe a favor once when a dispute arose over where the property line was, and Dad happened to be visiting with Joe on the day the survey had been done. Dad came into court to testify for Joe, and in return for this Joe built my dad a fish house so he didn't have to keep hauling the old shelter to and fro.

The fish house was placed in the same spot at the beginning of each winter. Father was precise in his winter fishing. In order to be as accurate as possible, he marked the spot, which was then lined up with a spot on the opposite shore. Then Dad would march off the same number of carefully measured steps that would place the fish house in just the right spot. One winter, one of Joe's boys got the house a few feet off from where it was supposed to be. It didn't take Dad long to realize how much a few feet can mean to the production of a fish house. After a week of substandard production the house was moved to where it always was, and fishing returned to normal.

The house was heated by the same old kerosene stove that provided heat for the canvas shelter. In those days there just weren't many stoves on the market that worked well enough to satisfy Dad, so he took an old four-burner kerosene kitchen stove, and modified it to one burner. The homemade stove worked better than any store-bought stove, and fit nicely in an old wooden dynamite box from the mine, which made a fine case for the cut down kerosene stove. Dad didn't quit fishing when the sun went down, so light came from an old red Coleman Lantern that had provided reliable illumination for many years. On his days off, he would pack a lunch, brew up a thermos of coffee, made sure there were good batteries in his portable radio, and place everything in a small packsack that was carried out to the car. Winter was the only time Dad used minnows, which he kept lively in an insulated bucket whose water was religiously changed to keep everyone in good shape.

Ice fishing wasn't my idea of cutting-edge excitement, but every now and then I would head down to the lake to join him for an afternoon of fishing. I can still see him sitting there on that old dynamite box watching his bobber carefully for any sign of a hungry walleye nibbling on an anxious minnow. I can see him in his flannel shirt, listening to the radio, sipping a cup of hot coffee, looking at his fishing hole as if it were a television. He was the picture of contentment. It didn't seem to matter whether Dad caught anything or not, and he never let getting skunked spoil his time out in front of Joe Buck's hanger.

Most of my father's fish house adventures don't stand out in my memory, but there were a few times when he came home with a mess of extremely nice fish that stood out from the rest. My father was commissioned to catch a dinner of fish for the mayor, who was entertaining the governor. The governor was hungry for a meal of fresh walleye. It was a mission Dad was happy to succeed at, and it surely didn't hurt his standing at city hall.

Of all the times Dad spent on the ice, I think the time which stands out the most in my mind was the time Joe Buchner brought Dad home – the night Father fell off the wagon.

Like most people in my family, Father wasn't good with alcohol. Perhaps what makes this instance stand out is that it was unusual for Dad to mix fishing and drinking. The old days when he would guide gangsters on American Agnes, and get gassed with button men trying to make themselves scarce, were long in the past. I think the reason he didn't mix the two was that he was affected by even the slightest amounts of anything fermented. In a town famed for men who could carry a heavy load of booze and not show any effect, my dad was a lightweight. By the time this story was being lived out, Dad had reached the conclusion after years of research, that he just wasn't any good at it, so for the most part he was staying sober. The last thing anyone expected was for Father to fall off the wagon in the fish house.

It was toward the end of February, the evening of what had been an almost perfect winter day. Dad left that morning and it wasn't uncommon for him to stay to eight o'clock if the fish were biting. Neither Mother nor I was surprised that he wasn't home for supper. Auntie Evie was over visiting with mother, when their visit was interrupted by a knock on our kitchen door. I went to the door, and there stood Joe Buchner. When I asked Joe what he was doing at our house, he told me that he had Dad in the back of the truck, and he needed my help in getting him in the house. By that time the women had come into the kitchen. Mother asked what had happened, and if there was anything wrong.

I can still hear Joe Buck trying to explain what had happened down at the fish house. "Don't be too hard on the old boy, Alice, he didn't mean for any of this to happen."

"He's drunk isn't he?" said Mother in a pinched and terse voice. "Go out to the truck and help Mr. Buchner bring in your father, Michael."

I slipped on my shoes and coat and walked out to the truck with Joe. I was surprised when I saw him lower the tailgate, but not half as surprised as when I looked in the box of the truck. There lay Father stretched out like a mackerel on ice.

"What's he doing in the back of the truck?" I asked.

"He fell out of the fish house this afternoon and fell into a puddle of water. I didn't find him until after sundown, and by that time he had started to freeze in. Had to chop him out, and by the time I got him out to the truck the legs of his flight suit were frozen stiff, and I couldn't fit him in the cab. That's why I put him in the box."

"Do you think he's ok?" I asked. Joe responded by saying he thought Dad would be all right, because flight suits were meant to keep you warm even when wet, but that we should get him in soon just in case.

We slid him out of the back of the truck, and he was so solid by this time that you could almost stand him up, and we ended up dragging him in backwards, with me under one arm and Joe under the other. When we got into the kitchen, Mother had seen enough and she did what she did whenever she faced a situation like this. She put on her coat, slammed out of the house, and headed to the church to collect herself. Joe and I stood there with Auntie Evie.

Then I heard a sound that I never expected to hear at such a moment. It was a giggle that had come up from a deep place within my aunt as she stood looking at Dad. She had managed to hold it in long enough for her sister to slam out of the house. Soon it was joined from a good-natured chuckle from Joe Buchner, and before long the three of us laughed until it hurt.

"I've seen Checker with a load on before, but this gives a whole new meaning to the term stiff as a board," said my broadly smiling aunt. "What happened to get him started today? It's not like him to drink when he's down at the lake, Joe."

"Well, it's like I was trying to tell Alice when I came in,

it really wasn't Checker's fault. There was this retired army colonel who I met at coffee this morning who wanted to do some fishing. I told him how well Checker does in front of the hanger, and I invited him to come down for the afternoon. The colonel was over at Checker's house learning the secrets of the trade. I found out later that he had a bottle of fine sipping whiskey with him. The colonel didn't know that Checker got drunk real easy, and I imagine Checker didn't want to refuse an offer kindly meant. It was just about dark when the colonel stopped in to thank me by offering me a drink. Good thing he did, or I would have never thought to go and check on Checker. Let's slide him into the living room, Mikey."

My aunt went into the living room and took the blanket off the sofa and spread it out on the floor. Joe and I dragged the still frozen and immobile form of my father across the kitchen and laid him out on the living room floor. It was like parking a frozen car in a heated garage. "We'll turn up the heat and see if we can't get him thawed," smiled my aunt.

"How did he ever end up out on the ice?" she asked Joe.

"Best as I can figure, I think he was going to look out the fish house door to see what time it was, and he just sort of keeled over. It was warm enough to have melted things in front of the house, but by the time I got there things had started to firm up again, and I had to do some fancy chiseling to get him freed up."

My aunt invited Joe to stay for a cup of coffee before he gave me a ride down to the hanger so I could drive Father's car home. On the way down to the lake he told me not to be too hard on the old boy, because he would feel pretty bad about it come morning, when he had to face Mother's cold and quiet wrath.

If there was a lesson that I took away from the whole thing, it was the truth Mark Twain had written. Humor was often times a bad thing happening to someone else, and there was no humor in heaven. The incident was never mentioned in our house, but every now and then Joe and I would share a laugh when we looked back on it. I think my lesson was not the only one learned, because it was the first and last time Dad ever took a drink at the fish house. On those rare occasions when anyone offered him a drink, Dad would look down at his fish hole and say he never mixed business with pleasure.

Flowers for Sally

On a beautiful late summer afternoon, Mother and I were at the church getting the altar ready for Sunday. Of Mother's many duties at church, she took great pride in preparing her altar each week. Most of the time she decorated it with flowers, and in the summer mother had permission from some of the town's best gardeners to take blooms from their gardens and place them on what she liked to refer to as God's altar. In the off season she would get Father to head out into the woods to help in her work. In the spring Dad would bring her the first and finest pussy willows, and in the autumn he would bring her colored leaves and asters. I liked being in the church in the late afternoon. For some reason the main windows of the sanctuary faced north and west, but they built the manse due west of the church, which effectively blocked most of the afternoon sun. I liked the late afternoon, especially in the summer, because it was the only time the sun would come through the gold and white stained glass windows. I liked to see the church take on a golden glow at the end of the day.

We were waiting there in order to pass inspection. About half the Sundays during the year, the flowers on the altar were dedicated to the memory of Sally Richards. Whenever that was the case, her father Ben would come to give his approval. Ben Richards was the superintendent of the Zenith Mine where my father worked, and no one ever called him Ben. Dad liked to say that you could B.S. a lot of people, but you couldn't B.S. B. S. Richards. Richards was a powerful man in town, who demanded respect. He was married to a wonderful woman named Jesse who suffered from cancer of the face, which would eventually eat her face away and finally kill her. At first, before things got too bad, she would come to church wearing a scarf. Finally she stopped coming to church, and would only visit with people over the phone. Shortly before she died, I called her and asked if Mother and I could come for a visit. She thanked me, but told me she was not receiving visitors. I think Ben Richards was the loneliest man I knew after Jesse died.

Jesse's skin cancer wasn't the only sorrow the Richards family had to deal with. Years ago their daughter Sally went to Alaska to teach school, and she returned one summer to tell her parents that she had fallen in love and wanted to get married. According to the story Mother told me, the man Sally selected was a Native Alaskan who didn't pass muster with Ben Richards. Angry words were exchanged between father and daughter. Sally went back to Alaska determined to marry the man she loved. On the return trip, the plane in which she traveled crashed and Sally Richards was killed. It was one of those deep wounds that a person never really gets over, which is why there were so many flower arrangements on the church altar dedicated to her memory. It was a way for Ben Richards to deal with the lingering guilt over the forever unresolved situation with Sally.

The sun dipped below the horizon when the church door opened and in walked Ben Richards. He was an imposing figure, even as an old man. He carried himself well, standing over six feet tall, mostly bald, with a deep bass voice, and dark-framed glasses. Ben Richards said hello to Mother and me, and then he walked slowly up to the altar.

I thought about the story my dad told me about one of the men who had advanced to a foreman's job. The foreman started to call Ben Richards by his first name. Ben Richards stopped him cold. He was Mr. Richards, not Ben, and Dad said that was the only time he ever heard anyone address Mr. Richards by his first name. I remember asking Mother's friend Nile what it was like having a mine superintendent in our church. Nile responded by saying, "Honey, there was this new gal who didn't know how things worked, and when we ended up one salad short for the church luncheon, the new gal said, 'Why don't we just call Jesse Richards?' and I told her that up here you didn't call Jesse Richards, she called you." It was all a matter of respect.

"Aren't the flowers lovely this summer, Mr. Richards?" asked Mother. Ben Richards turned to her and agreed with Mother's assessment of the summer flowers.

"Wouldn't Sally and Jesse be pleased with this Sunday's altar?" Mother looked at the flowers that sat in what was known to everyone in the church as Sally's vase.

"Yes Alice," responded Ben Richards. "I only wish they could be standing here with us to see for themselves."

"Oh, I think they're both looking down on us from heaven," answered Mother.

Ben Richards turned to my mother and said, "Alice, would you do me a favor and call me Ben."

I can still see the surprised look that crossed my mother's face. She made a couple of attempts at saying the word Ben, but the word stuck in her mouth and wouldn't come out. The closest she could come to saying the word was a sheep-like *bah, bah, bah* sound.

She finally looked up at that lonely man, and told him that she couldn't bring herself to call him anything but Mr. Richards. I remember watching a sad look cross his face. Then he looked at Mother and told her he understood that some things just weren't meant to be. He patted Mother on the shoulder, thanked her for all that she had done for Jesse and Sally over the years, and turned and walked down the center aisle of the church and out of the sanctuary.

"Why couldn't you call him Ben?" I asked.

"Oh Michael. He's been Mr. Richards for so long now, that I just couldn't call him by his first name. It didn't feel right."

"I feel sorry for him," I said.

She thought for a moment. "Yes, I feel sorry for him

too. Neither he nor Jesse ever got over Sally's death and now that Jesse is gone, I think Ben Richards is just about the loneliest person I know. He worked so hard keeping people at a distance, that now he's all alone without a real friend in the world. It's one of the costs of power, Michael. The more power you get, the more it isolates you from people. Then you get old and retire, and the power is gone, and you end up like Ben Richards – a lonely old man."

It has been many years since that summer afternoon, but whenever I am in church, and look at flowers on the altar, I travel back in time. I think about my mother, and Ben Richards standing in the fading light of a summer afternoon, looking at flowers for Sally.

Struck By Lightning

I must have gone past the tree dozens of times, but I never noticed it. The tree in question was a healthy white pine that stood on the side of the branch of the Trezona Trail. The Trezona Trail was named after Captain Charlie Trezona, and it runs just over four miles around Miners Lake. It is a fine trail. Before the snow comes, I spend a lot of time either biking or hiking on that trail. When the snow comes, I strap on my old wood skis to satisfy my Norwegian genetics.

I must have gone past that tree dozens of times, but I never noticed it. It was a normal good-sized white pine. We don't think about it, but it isn't the normal things we remember. We remember the things that stand out, and the thing that finally made this tree stand out was when it got hit by lightning.

I passed by the tree the day before it was set apart from all the other trees around it. The tree stood by the side of a pond. The pond used to be a hunting ground for blue herons, and a home for painted turtles. I had enjoyed the pond for years, but during that time it had shrunk to half its size. There had been some roadwork done in the area, and I still am not sure if the pond is getting smaller because someone installed better drainage, or if the pond is shrinking because the world is getting warmer. The next day I passed the same spot, and my entire focus changed.

The pine – that yesterday had been nothing out of the ordinary – had been set apart. A late season October thunderstorm passed through the night before, and sometime during that storm the pine had suffered a tremendous blow. About a third of the southeast side of the pine had exploded, and pieces of bone-white wood were scattered as far as forty feet in front of the pine. I knew what had happened; the tree had been struck by lightning, and the heat from the lightning had caused so much steam in the tree that the tree just exploded. I stood there in the early morning sunshine watching the steam come off the tree. Closer to the tree you could see the orange scar, from lightning, that ran down the center of the tree.

The first thing I thought about when I saw that scar was the time I was hit by lightning. You never forget once you've been hit by a bolt of lightning, and are lucky enough to write about it over thirty years later. I was running Bill Rom's canoe base on Moose Lake. It was the summer of 1973 and I was in my third year of college. The reason the day stands out in my mind was on account of the lightning. The day started off hot and muggy, and you could feel things building. By evening, the sun had sent enough moisture aloft that there were huge banks of clouds moving in from the east. I think most people that die in the Boundary Waters die by drowning, but lightning strikes are a close second. Mark Twain wrote that it wasn't that the world was full of fools, it was just that lightning wasn't distributed right, and that's the truth.

Most of the people that I knew that drowned could have been saved easily. They were either not wearing a life jacket when they dumped their canoe, or they did something dumb such as swimming in front of a rapids. But with lightning most of the time it's as it was with the pine; being in the wrong place at the wrong time. Such as when the two brothers were camping with their sons on Ensign Lake. One of my friends was dropping off a party at the Ensign Portage when these two guys came stumbling down the trail. He thought they were drunk at first, but then he knew they were in shock. They had been camped under this average-sized tree when it was hit. The one brother and son were killed. The other two survived because they had plastic zippers in their sleeping bags, while the other two had metal ones. Sometimes life is like that.

The night I was hit by lightning there was a big group of boy scouts up from someplace in Oklahoma. Like most of the people who came up to canoe in the Boundary Waters, the closest they had been to a canoe was watching the movie *Deliverance*. In an effort to help them get their paddles wet, I would let them have the canoes free of charge the evening before they went out. It didn't cost the company a dime, and it gave people a chance to paddle around in front of the canoe base, before they had to set out in the morning. I lived in a small trailer on the shore of the lake, and it was all a young bachelor could ask. It had a living room, kitchen, a bathroom, and bedroom; all so small that there wouldn't ever be a thought of having to share it with anyone but somebody you wanted. The guy that ran the base the year before painted the words Sleepy Hollow on it, and that sounded ok to me.

I watched the clouds start to build in the sky, and it was easy to see what was going to be coming, so I got out in my boat in order to call in my flotilla of voyageurs. I remember feeling like being some kind of sheep-herding dog, and I was amazed at how far some of them had gotten away from the canoe base. By the time I got everyone ashore and out of harm's way, the first bolts of lightning were forking down, and there was thunder rolling over the lakes. I felt lucky to have gotten in ahead of the rain, and I felt good that all my people were safely on shore.

Regular phones hadn't been installed on Moose Lake in 1973 and communication with the outside world was done with a mobile phone. In order for the phone to work over such a distance, you needed a long whip antenna. In a moment that I can still see clearly, I had just slipped the key into the padlock on the door to the trailer when this bolt of lightning, which I can still see and feel, hit the antenna.

The next thing I remember was being slapped on the face. I was lying over thirty feet from the trailer, holding the stump of a key in my hand. I was soaking wet, and the guy that was slapping my face said that they watched me get hit, and they both thought I was a gone goose. The trailer door was wide open, and the lock and other half of the key were nowhere to be found. About a week later a friend of mine stood in front of the door of the trailer, and he took a rock and tossed it as far as he could over his shoulder. Sure enough, after poking around in the woods, we found the lock with the key in it. It had been cut by lightning.

When the lightning hit the antenna and ran down to where I held the key in the lock, the shock of the bolt turned the key in the lock which broke the circuit with the lightning bolt. It knocked me a good thirty feet and the lock went twice that far. There was a tingling feeling all over my body, and I felt sure that if I held a light bulb in my hand it would have lit up.

I have heard people say that someone is never quite the same after they have been hit by lightning, and I don't doubt it's true. Once someone asked me if I was afraid of thunderstorms, and I told them they held no fear for me. I have great respect for lightning, and I don't go out of my way looking for trouble.

Mouse Turds and Mike Kelly

My great grandfather never learned to like an automobile. Like many men who had grown up with the horse and buggy, Bill Labeau never quite got the hang of mastering the horseless carriage. Not wanting to seem as if the world was leaving him behind, he purchased a brand new Chevrolet, but after a few attempts to master the metallic monster the car stayed in the garage. Dad wasn't sure what the problem was, but he thought it was a matter of not being able to get the thing to shift into reverse. When the old man almost put the car through the back of the garage, that was it for Bill Labeau and the automobile. The car would stay there for a number of years until his grandson Chester was old enough to take it out on the road. Even then the old man wasn't aware that his car was at last being put to good use. Chester and his friends would push the car out of the garage and when they got it a safe distance from home, they would unhook the speedometer, so his grandfather wouldn't catch them by the miles. While most of the world had traded the tack room for the garage, you would still see Bill Labeau behind a team of horses, safe and secure in the seat of a buggy.

Bill Labeau was one of the first old settlers. He was one of the French-Canadian packers who came with Martin and William Patterson back in the spring of 1885, before there was anything here other than an Indian village on Shagawa Lake. He and his wife Mary Ellen had come with Captain Morcomb from Michigan to work at the Minnesota Mine the year before, and they had been there when the first train of iron left for the loading docks on Lake Superior. Their one claim to local fame came in June of that year when Mary Ellen gave birth to a son William, who was the first white child born north of Duluth.

Bill Labeau didn't care to work underground, so as soon as the village and then city of Ely was incorporated, he served as Sargent of Police and was a loyal member of the local fire department. He had seen the start of the big logging, which settled in a place named Winton, named after the son-in-law of one of the big lumber companies. Now in the mid-1920s, Bill Labeau had seen the big lumber companies close. He remembered the companies saying that they would never be able to log off all the timber, but in this case they never numbered less than thirty years.

But Ely was an iron town whose special ore was a vital ingredient to how America made steel, and Bill Labeau knew that the mining was destined to outlive him. He was happy about that, because he had lived in some small mining locations in the Upper Peninsula of Michigan. He once told his grandson that he was glad that the town would outlive him, and not vice versa.

Over the years he got to know everyone. He was one of the founding members of the Old Settlers Association that formed in 1914 when someone noticed that quite a number of old settlers had already crossed over and were pushing up daisies. The town's first cemetery was located in a big bank of gravel and sand that the glaciers had put there a few thousand years back, which sat just to the southwest of town. That sand and gravel bank was worth thousands of dollars as the town started to grow and roads started to be built. Someone dug up to the edge of what was referred to as Smoke's Farm, in honor of Joe Smoke. Joe got the honor because his farm was furthest out from town, and stood before the cemetery gate. That's when the trouble started.

The first good rain of the season brought a number of the old settlers tumbling out of the sandbank. When one of the bodies that came out turned out to be one of the town's most notorious drinkers, the town enjoyed a dark laugh about never having been able to keep him out of the taverns. They ended up putting up a large wooden charnel box so they had somewhere to keep the disinterred while the town council debated the matter. The city ended up buying land about a mile east of town, which is still receiving occupants to the present. The Smokes ended up leaving town, and many were fond of commenting that the town had run out of Smokes, but there was another family in town by the name of Smuk, so the new place, complete with a mass grave for the people in the charnel box, became Smuk's farm in their honor.

The Old Settlers Club got together that summer as dozens of the old timers talked about the old days over steaming bowls of lumberjack stew called boyja. They talked about all that they had seen from the start of the mining back in the 1880s, when everyone knew everyone else. They talked about the panic of 1892 when it looked as if the plug had been pulled on the town. It was a bad stretch of time that saw three mines shut down and fill up with water, and the town was down to just the Chandler Mine. Many people pulled up stakes and headed back to where they came from. Things started to pick up again in '97 when Henry L. Oliver came to town representing none other than Andrew Carnegie with a great fat check book that held enough money to buy the Pioneer Mine from a group of Duluth investors. The old timers talked about the turn of the century when Carnegie joined forces with Rockefeller and Morgan, and gave birth to the United States Steel Corporation. They lamented all the changes that took place in the first decade of the new century when the town was overrun by thousands of foreigners who came to work in the mines, and their little town became a city of strangers. The Old Settlers Association still meets every summer, and it's interesting to know that the conversation hasn't changed all that much with the passing years.

One of Bill Labeau's favorite old settlers was a trapper named Mike Kelly. During the logging days Mike would flesh out his trapping income by hunting for the lumber camps, and put up a supply of what was referred to as pine beef. Deer weren't native to this part of the state, so Mike Kelly hunted moose and caribou for the camps. With hundreds of men working in the woods it didn't take long to wipe out all the caribou, and most of the moose. Things became so desperate for the wolves that Mike Kelly remembered winters when they replaced the heavy horses with mules, because wolves started to attack tote teams. Horses are terrified of wolves, but mules weren't the least afraid of wolves, and they would give a hungry wolf a good kick from a hoof filled with bad intent. Things got so bad the state put a stop to the practice of harvesting pine beef after that, but most of the damage had been done. The woodland caribou were gone from the state, replaced by white-tailed deer, and it would take the moose years to recover. It wasn't that people such as Mike Kelly were bad; everything seemed so big back then that people believed they would never run out of it.

One fall, Mike dropped a good-sized cow moose only to find out she had twin calves, which made him feel dreadful. Not wanting to see the twin moose go into some logger's stew pot, he roped them and led them into town, which caused quite a stir. One of the people he met that day was Ed Crossman, who owned a saloon and restaurant in town. When Ed asked Mike what he was going to do with the moose calves, Mike said he really wasn't sure. Ed offered to buy them, and he and Mike struck a deal. Ed Crossman became the proud owner of two moose, and Mike Kelly had a line of credit at Crossman's Saloon and Buffet.

Ed Crossman took the moose down to his farm where he trained them to pull a cutter during the winter of 1905. Even though it was Ed who trained them, they would only work for Ed's wife, and if she wasn't on the other end of the reigns they wouldn't budge an inch. You can still see the picture of those two moose hitched up to a cutter pulling two women over the frozen streets of Ely. Nobody knows for sure just what happed, but one of the moose disappeared that spring, and there was some talk that it was shot and ended up in someone's stew pot. The other moose was broken hearted by the loss of its sister, and ended up wasting away that spring from what looked to be extreme loneliness.

If Mike Kelly had a defining feature, it was a crooked right arm. One summer Mike was out picking blueberries when a mean-tempered black bear took objection to Mike's invasion of what the bear considered to be its home turf. The bruin ended the dispute by running Mike up a white pine. Mike told his friends he was up in that pine for a considerable period of time while that big old bear took its sweet time cleaning up the berry patch. When the bear finally finished up and left, Mike started back down, but a branch broke underneath him and he fell a good ten feet to the ground. In order to break his fall Mike put out his arms, and that's how he ended up breaking his right arm. It was a long way to town, so when Mike got back to his shack, he bound his arm to his body with an old make-do sling. He left it that way and went about his business the best he could until his arm healed up enough to take it out of the sling. The only problem was his arm healed crooked and he could never straighten his right arm again. When the doctor suggested re-breaking the arm and starting over, Mike Kelly decided he could handle living with one crooked arm that was still quite useful.

One of my father's most vivid memories of Mike Kelly was the morning that my father and his grandfather rented a buggy from the Dinsmore Livery Stable, packed a picnic lunch, and headed out to visit his old friend. Like many of the old trappers, Mike Kelly lived alone in a cabin near Birch Lake Dam that had once been used by the loggers, but had been deserted when the loggers headed towards the big woods out west. Like many of the men who had spent mostly solitary lives out in the woods, Mike Kelly tried living with a few of the other old trappers in a cost-saving venture. Most of the experiments in shared living failed, because the men had become so set in their ways that they couldn't stand any other habits but their own. They mostly lived alone.

It was a ten-mile ride from Ely out to Birch Lake. Spring was in full swing as they rode along the dirt road, which ran just over twenty miles to where the last of the big logging camps had been located up on the Stony River. Mike Kelly lived in one of the line cabins that were strung out along the length of the road. Ten miles doesn't seem like much to anyone who can hop in a car, but when a skinner was moving a big load of logs with a team of heavy horses, it was a long way. They never knew just how far they would get, so they strung out a series of cabins and barns along the road to provide safe harbor for men and horses on a cold winter night. When the work was finished, they left everything to time, and to people like Mike Kelly.

All told, it took my father and grandfather over two hours to do those ten miles, and when a car would shoot by the buggy like a comet shooting through the night sky, Chester thought about time, and how everything had changed with the arrival of the automobile. Though he didn't know it then, this would be the last horse and buggy ride he would take with his grandfather, and the last time he would ever think of ten miles the same way again.

Mike Kelly was glad to see them, and made them both feel welcome. You couldn't say that he rolled out the red carpet, because there weren't any carpets to roll out, red or otherwise, but he brewed up a pot of green tea in honor of the occasion, and then he and Bill Labeau sat down to visit. Mike Kelly was about the happiest man alive when he found out that Mary Ellen had loaded the picnic basket with some of her canned fruit. Like most bachelors he missed out on things like home bottled fruit, so the simple gift of sweetness meant the world to him. The men spent most of the day visiting. Mike wanted to know all that was happening around town, and then the two old friends digressed into talking about the old days, and some of the adventures they had shared over the years. Chester spent the day doing what boys do. He explored the old horse barn that still held on to the smell of the horses that had once stayed there. Later he borrowed one of Mike's old cane poles, dug up some worms, and tried his hand at a little fishing until his grandfather called, and told him that Mike had invited them to stay for supper.

When he got up to the cabin he found his grandfather sitting at the table sipping a cup of green tea, while Mike Kelly was busy in the kitchen getting supper ready. Chester watched as the crooked-armed old man took out a canvas sack that contained a good-sized slab of salt pork. That slab of pork was about as far gone as a piece of meat could go, and still be fit to eat. It had greened up a bit around the edges. Mike trimmed off some of the greener parts and tossed them out the open window for the Whiskey Jacks who waited eagerly for their rewards. The rest of the slices were soon sizzling in a cast iron skillet, which sat on the stove next to a big pot of boiling water where Mike Kelly had dropped a half dozen spuds. The old man went over to the flour barrel and scooped up a few cups into a big wooden mixing bowl. The boy could see that the mice had been in the barrel, and he could clearly see the small dark mouse turds that were mixed in with the flour. The next thing he expected to see Mike Kelly do was to get out a flour sifter like the women did at home, but the old trapper had long passed the point of worrying about a few mouse turds.

Chester didn't know it then, but Mike Kelly was whipping up a batch of griddle cakes called bannock that people such as Mike Kelly counted on as a staple food. Mike placed another heavy black iron pan on the surface of the cook stove, greased it up, and then scooped the batter into the pan. Chester realized that a two-inch-thick pancake covered the entire pan. When he asked Mike what kind of syrup he was going to put on the bannock, both men laughed. "Don't got no syrup, boy, but we'll fix her up with a little gravy and things will be just fine," said the old man in a friendly voice. Chester looked up at his grandfather and gave him a pleading look, silently asking if he really had to eat the supper that would be placed before him. His grandfather looked down at him with a stern look, and with one terse nod conveyed the message that any insult to the hospitality of his old friend would not be welcomed. Chester gulped a silent gulp, and settled himself to the grim task ahead.

Mike dished everyone up from the stove, and soon there

were three plates on the table, each with two spuds, salt pork, and a pie-sized piece of bannock. Just as Chester was about to take his first bite, the old man stopped him by saying, "Wait sonny, you can't start yet, you ain't had none of the gravy." And with that said, he walked back to the stove, and reached up for a dusty old cream pitcher that he filled with the liquid fat that had cooked off the salt pork. Then he walked back to the table and proudly poured a liberal amount over the food on the boy's plate.

"There you are son, now you're all fixed up with the gravy."

Chester took one last gulp, breathed a deep breath, and then dug into a meal he would remember the rest of his life. When he finished the last bite the old man smiled over at Chester and said that if he had known just how hungry Chester was, he would have thrown an extra spud in the pot. Chester thanked the old man and told him that if he were to eat another bite he would probably burst. Mike Kelly grinned from ear to ear, basking in the reflective glow that all cooks deserve when they see that their preparations were well received. When Chester looked over at his grandfather, he was graced with a favorable nod.

The day was pretty well spent when they took their leave of Mike Kelly. Grandfather lit the lights on the buggy before they headed back to town. There was a chill in the evening air. As they pulled away from the front of the shack, Bill Labeau turned around to give his old friend one last wave, and to reach for the blanket that was neatly folded in the back of the buggy. He turned back to the open road, and spread the blanket across the knees of himself and his grandson who was holding the reigns and driving the show.

"Does he eat like that all the time?" asked Chester.

"Don't be so stupid, boy. If we wouldn't have been there he would have cooked up one thing, but he never would have cooked all three. It didn't seem much to you, because you've been spoiled by the company of women, but Mike Kelly gave you as good as he had, and you mustn't ever forget it. A man's just got to have the good sense to know when the going don't get no better."

Years later, when we sat down to one of Mother's new healthful dinners – Spanish rice – I thought about what Dad had told me about dining with Mike Kelly. Mother was on a diet that frowned on potatoes in any form, so we were looking for alternatives. "Some men are born to rice, Michael, and others have rice thrust upon them," said Father as he looked down on a meal, the likes of which he had never seen before. This was a time when life was still simple. Rice was white, and it had a black man on the box named Uncle Ben. The world was black and white. Rice was white, and Uncle Ben wasn't. There just weren't different kinds of things. Apples were apples, and oranges were oranges; take it or leave it.

Here I was, faced with the same dilemma, which had confronted my father years before. To eat, or not to eat, that is the question, and looking down at my plate, it was indeed a profound question. There on my plate sat a concoction the likes of which I had never seen before. It was one of Mother's few efforts in creative cooking, and Dad and I were both grateful for that. In a burst of Norwegian culinary creativity, Mother had created something almost as memorable as the supper Mike Kelly had thrown together for my father years before.

In an effort to look good for her men, Mother was going on a diet. In the generous spirit of imparting the true meaning of walking in someone else's shoes, Mother allowed us to walk her walk by partaking from her bill of fare. In her effort to look good, Mother had declared war on starch, and potatoes had become a dirty word. There on my plate sat a combination of Uncle Ben's Rice, Elliot Bacon, and chopped onion, all lovingly simmered in two cans of Campbell's Tomato Soup. I looked into my father's eyes, and saw the boy who still remembered Mike Kelly. I didn't say a word, and ate the whole plateful of what proved to be one of my most memorable meals.

When I was done with supper, Mother beamed and lamented that if she knew how much we liked Spanish rice, she would have made more. Father and I rolled our eyes to heaven and uttered a silent prayer. When Mother went into the other room, Dad looked at me and said, "This is worse than mouse turds and Mike Kelly." From that meal on, part of my life has been bracketed by Mike Kelly's mouse turds and Mother's Spanish rice. If given my druthers I would advise anyone to damn the Spanish rice, and opt for the mouse turds.

Prayer Candles

None of us could believe our eyes when Marshall rode up to the ball field on a brand new blue bicycle. It had a light, a built-in horn, and streamers coming from the handlebars. It was a Schwinn, and it was beautiful.

"How did you get it?" Richard asked.

"Prayer candles," Marshall answered.

"What's a prayer candle?" I asked.

"You Protestants don't know nothing," shot back Marshall. "You know those red candles that sit up front, at the side of our church?"

"Yes. What about them?"

"Those are the prayer candles," said Marshall. "When you want to say a prayer, all you've got to do is pay your money and light a candle. There are two sizes. The small candles cost a dime, and the big candle costs a dollar. Just before you light the candle, you say the prayer you want prayed, and as long as that candle burns your prayer is being prayed to God."

This was a new thing to me. We didn't have prayer candles at the Presbyterian Church.

"Do you mean to tell me that you really believe that you can light a candle and have it say a prayer for you?" asked Richard, who was a Lutheran.

"You see this bike?" said Marshall. Everyone on the ball field chimed in with a collective yes. "Every day last month I went to the church and paid my ten cents, lit my candle, and prayed for this bike. And here she is, and ain't she a beauty?" There she was all right, and she sure was a beauty. "I guess you might say I'm sitting on the proof," Marshall said proudly.

I wasn't sure I believed in a prayer candle, but I had my eye on a silver and black Schwinn bike that was sitting in the window of the hardware store. I knew that it would take me a long time to pay for it with money saved from my paper route, and I didn't want to wait all summer to get that bike. If Marshall was right, and it took him a month of prayers to get his new bike I figured the price to be right around three dollars. Me being a Presbyterian, it might take a little longer than it would for a Catholic, but I figured that even if it took a month longer for a Protestant it would still be worth the money. That's when I started lighting prayer candles.

Every afternoon just before supper I went into Saint Anthony's Church to light a prayer candle. I went in the late afternoon, because it was quiet. Father Mike and the nuns weren't around, and even though I didn't think I was doing anything wrong, I didn't want to call any attention to what I was doing. I thought that perhaps there might be some kind of a rule about Protestants lighting prayer candles, and I really wanted a new bike. There were more Catholics in town than Presbyterians, and walking into the Catholic Church for me was like entering a cathedral. The windows were set high near the ceiling, and the walls of the church were made of fine Italian marble. There were carved wooden figures along the walls of both sides of the church telling the story of the Crucifixion that my friend Marshall told me were called the Stations of the Cross.

I remember feeling cheated when I thought about my little church with its lone wooden cross in the front of the church, with the simple words "Love one another as I have loved you" carved in the altar. Why didn't we have prayer candles, or carvings along the walls of our church? What was wrong with having stained glass windows with real pictures on them? I told myself that if I got my new bike I was going to go back to the people in my church and tell them that we were really missing out by not having prayer candles. And if anyone needed proof, I would point to my new black and silver Schwinn bicycle as a testament to the power of prayer candles.

I made at least twenty trips to Saint Anthony's that month, before Father Mike happened to see me in the church and asked me what I was doing. I told him the truth, that I was there lighting a prayer candle, and that's as far as things went until I got home. When I walked through the back door of our house and into the kitchen, Mother was sitting at the table. She had her serious look on, and I wondered what was up.

"Is something wrong, Michael?" she asked.

"No mother, there's nothing wrong. Why do you ask?"

"I just got a call from Father Mike asking me why you were up at Saint Anthony's lighting a prayer candle."

It was one of the bad things about living in a small town where most everyone knew everyone else. You just couldn't do anything without someone calling your mom and dad, and telling them what you had done. It was like the time Mrs. Strom caught me stealing crab apples and turned the garden hose on me, and gave me a good soaking. By the time I got home, she had already called my mom to tell me why I was all wet, and I ended up grounded for the week. Like I say, it was hard to get away with anything when I was a boy. My dad's moral code was based on the simple premise that stealing was stupid to do in a place as small as Ely, because if you took something from someone else, everyone would know who's thing it was. The only thing you could do if you took something was to squirrel it away where it did no good to you, or anyone else. It was a practical thing that made sense to me. The world would be a much more honest place if we all lived in small towns.

I looked at my mother, and in the spirit of George Washington, I told her that I could not tell a lie. She told me to cut it out, and come to the point.

"I wanted a new bicycle," I said, "And Marshall told me he got his new bicycle by lighting prayer candles, so I've been going up to Saint Anthony's every afternoon and lighting a candle."

Mother told me to sit down at the kitchen table. "Michael, I'm not saying you did anything wrong by lighting a prayer candle, but we're Presbyterian, and we don't believe in prayer candles. If you want to say a prayer for a bike, then you should do it the way I taught you."

Every night when I was a boy we would say, "Now I lay me down to sleep, I pray the Lord my soul to keep. If I should die before I wake, I pray the Lord my soul to take." Then I would bless just about everyone I knew.

Mother looked at me and asked if I really thought that a bicycle was something I should be praying about anyway. "God helps those who help themselves," she said. Mother always liked to say things like that. "You've probably spent close to two dollars already this month lighting those candles, and wasting good money on a silly superstition. You start putting those dimes in a bank, and before you know it, you'll have enough money for a bike, and your prayers will have been answered. That's how you'll get what you want, by earning it."

About two months after that, the phone rang with bad news. One of Mother's good friends, Joe Mishmash, was trapped underground in a cave in at the Pioneer Mine, and no one knew if he was dead or alive. The next thing I knew we were pulling on our coats and heading up to Saint Anthony's Church. When we got into the church it was already getting dark, and I could hear women's voices chanting in unison. It took a moment before my eyes adjusted to the dim light in the church, but then I could see a group of women wearing black kerchiefs on there heads. They were all holding rosary beads in their hands, and they were chanting Hail Marys over and over again.

"What are they doing here?" I asked.

"They're praying, Michael. They always do when there is someone trapped underground. Most of those women have lost men to the mines, and they remember how terrible it was to have one of your men trapped underground. They will sit here and pray as long as the rescue miners are digging, and they will pray in shifts for as long as it takes."

Then we walked up the side aisle of the church to where the prayer candles were. Some of them were burning away in their red candleholders, and I thought they looked beautiful even if they didn't work. But then my mother did something I couldn't believe. She took a dollar bill out of her purse, pushed it into the collection box, and lit one of the big candles.

"I thought you told me that this was a silly superstition," I said as I looked at her by candlelight.

"Don't be stupid, Michael. My friend Joe is Catholic, and if this candle does any good at all for him, then it is a dollar well spent. And furthermore we're going to come here every day and light a candle until we know that Joe's all right."

There were times when you could discuss things with Mother, and then there were times like this when it was best not to press the point. I took a dime out of my pocket, lit a candle, and prayed for Joe Mishmash.

They found Joe Mishmash alive a few days later, and on my birthday I got that brand new silver and black Schwinn bicycle that I had admired for so long in the hardware store window. My older brother Tommy had been hired at one of the mines, and he bought it for me. I don't know for sure whether or not the prayer candles did Joe Mishmash or me any real good, and I'm not sure if they have prayer candles any more. But I still think it was a beautiful thought, and I'm sure all those dimes and dollars people put in the coin box over the years answered the prayers of a lot of needy people. In that respect it was all money well spent. One the most vivid memories I have of Saint Anthony's Catholic Church is standing with my mother on that day in the darkening sanctuary. The last light has gone from the windows, and we are standing by candlelight while women in black scarves say Hail Marys for the safety of a trapped miner. *Holy Mary, Mother of God, pray for us sinners now and at the hour...*

The Worst Thing You Ever Did

I never liked him from the first time I saw him, but in view of what happened later, maybe I'm lucky to be here at all. I knew him as Eric from Toledo. It was an early spring morning. I was on my cycle, taking a ride to the far side of Shagawa Lake to see my friend Ropey. Ice was still on the puddles as I rode down the Gold Mine Road, and I can still hear the sound of my bike tires breaking ice. They called it The Gold Mine Road, because back near the end of the 1890s they were convinced there was gold on the west end of the lake. They sunk a couple of shafts, but they never found any gold. If you drive down the road, and keep a sharp eye, you can see the piles of white chert still visible along the trail.

It was always a bit of an adventure for me to head out to the far side of the lake. Ropey was a lonesome bachelor. He bought land on the west end of the lake; land that we had fallen in love with when we were kids. He put up a couple of cabins to go along with the little shack with the small round woodstove. The shack stood on the top of the hill for what seemed to be forever.

One of the things that made it such fun was every time I paid a visit, every stray packsacker who drifted north would end up at Ropey's. I used to describe myself as a Richie Cunningham kind of a guy, but now it's more like Howard if the truth were told, so it was always an adventure to take a bike ride out to the far side.

That's why I wasn't surprised when I came around a

corner of the road and met someone walking toward me. He was a good-sized man standing well over six feet tall, and you could see at a distance that he was well put together. His hair was black and wavy, and he had deep brown eyes. But the thing that stood out even more was that he was carrying Ropey's twelve-gauge shotgun.

"Ropey isn't going to like you being out here shooting his ruffed grouse," I said, as I pulled to a stop a few feet in front of him.

"I'm staying with Ropey, and what's it to you what I'm doing out here?"

When I looked into those dark eyes, it was like looking into the eyes of a hawk. Looking into them made me feel as if I was looking into heart of a predator. There wasn't the least bit of warmth or humanity in those eyes. At that moment I became aware of the fact that I was dealing with a stranger carrying a shotgun, who seemed miffed that I had the temerity to question what he was doing. There have been few times in my life when I have felt a little fear in the pit of my stomach, and this was one of them. It was time for diplomacy, and I was smart enough to know it.

"All I'm trying to do is to tell you that you don't hunt ruffed grouse in the spring. The birds are on the nest now, and if you kill them there won't be any chicks hatched, and that will ruin the hunting next fall. Ropey would tell you the same thing." I told him my name, and that I was an old friend of Ropey.

He told me that he was Eric something-or-other, and that he had come north from Toledo, Ohio, to see what life on the edge of the wilderness was like. Eric told me that Ropey was out of town for a few days. I told him that it was nice meeting him. Then I turned my cycle around and headed back the way I came.

A few days later the phone rang and it was Ropey on the line, telling me he had made it home, and that I should take a ride out for a visit. The ride out was memorable for a couple of reasons. It was a beautiful May morning when I started west on my cycle. The ride out from town was all of fourteen miles round trip, so when I took the ride, I made sure that I had the time set aside to make a day of it. There was an outbreak of forest tent caterpillars that year, and when I stopped to take a drink from my bike bottle, I could hear small snapping sounds around me. It took me a few moments before I realized that the sound I was hearing was thousands of caterpillars munching their way through the forest, denuding every poplar and birch tree within marching distance. It is one of those events that make things stand out, and now many years later, I can still hear the small snapping sounds of thousands of tent caterpillars enjoying a little lunch.

When I pulled up to the cabin, the sun felt like melted butter on my back and shoulders as I walked down to the lake. A small group of people gathered around a fire, on which sat a huge black pot that was busily steaming away. Greetings were exchanged all around, and I asked them what was cooking in the pot.

"Turtle," answered Ropey. "Came in after a stringer of fish this morning. Thought he was going to have himself a little breakfast, so we decided to invite him to stay to dinner." Ropey grinned. He said things should be ready for the table in about an hour or so, and I knew how good fresh cooked turtle was, with its multiple kinds of meat, so I pulled up a stump and basked in the sunshine. Every now and then the wind would blow the smell of cooking turtle and wood smoke my way, which lent added flavor to the day.

Eric was sitting across from me, and I asked him what he was planning on doing with himself. He told me he wanted to throw together some gear, head out in the woods, live off the land, and maybe start himself a trap line. There was a time when people could come up to Ely and do that, but those times were long past. I asked him what kind of equipment he had that would handle a northern winter where things often get down to forty below or better. He walked over to the cabin and came back with a pair of thinly insulated hunting boots. I looked at those boots and told Eric that anyone who knew anything about this country could tell him those boots wouldn't be up to the job. What he needed was a pair of packs or mukluks, and lots of wool socks.

He snorted at me, laughed, and told me that he was a big boy who was able to take care of himself. I was getting a little worked up by this time, and I told him that he should start paying attention to how things are properly done, or he would never learn anything. I pointed out over the water and told him that the lake looked pretty warm and friendly today, but I had seen her when she was all churned up by a big wind, and then she wasn't so nice. I told him this was a dangerous country to underestimate, and that more than one person came to grief because of it. The conversation drifted to other topics, and before long we all sat down to a fine turtle dinner. It was the last time I saw Eric from Toledo.

About a week later, I was enjoying a morning cup of coffee when the phone rang. It was Ropey's dad Joe, and he wanted to know if I had seen Ropey. I told Joe that I hadn't seen him for a few days and I asked Joe what was up. We talked about the big wind that clippered through yesterday, and early this morning they found Ropey's boat drifting upside down on the other end of the lake. Ropey lived on one of the most sheltered bays on Shagawa Lake, and both Joe and I knew that it wasn't likely that the boat could have blown to that end of the lake unless someone had taken it out of the bay and onto the lake proper. It was one of those moments when you felt one of those sinking feelings deep inside, where you hoped for the best, and feared the worst.

Just then, who should pull into the yard but Ropey. I told Joe that whoever took out the boat, it wasn't his boy down on the bottom of the lake. I told Joe I would tell Ropey what had happened, and that we would head out to the cabin to see if we could solve the mystery. I shared what I knew about the boat with Ropey, and he told me the only person out at the shack was Eric. We both feared the worst.

We started yelling his name as soon as we got out of the car, but we got no response. When we entered the cabin, we looked over at Eric's bunk, which was sitting unused in the sunshine coming in through the window. A brand new green camouflaged sterns-like jacket lay on the bed. We both knew at that moment that Eric was dead.

"I wonder what made him take the boat out in a wind like that?" I asked.

"Maybe he ran out of smokes," Ropey replied. A quick glance at the table showed us that there was still a half carton of cigarettes, which ruled out that option.

"I think we ought to head to town and start asking everyone we know if they happened to see Eric, so we can find if they know why he came to town."

Ropey nodded a silent yes. We headed back up the road to where the car was parked and started towards Ely. We split up when we got to town. The first two people I talked to hadn't seen Eric, but then I ran into Mikey Niblin.

If there was anyone who had loser written on him, it was Mike Niblin. When his parents saw Mikey coming to grief in the Twin Cities, they thought the best thing to do was to change Mike's environment, so they sent him as far north as they could. They thought that the drugs that their son loved too much wouldn't be as accessible in a place as remote as Ely. They could have sent him anywhere, but Mikey was going to do what he was going to do, and he found all he needed to right on the edge of the wilderness. There was no getting Mikey away from what he loved best. He was in his late twenties when I first met him, and in the course of a year or two, I watched him pawn just about everything he owned in order to support a habit that was bigger than its owner. Mikey reached the point in his life when he started stealing. Ropey came home early one day and caught him going through the drawers of his cabin, and Mikey was banned from the shack.

I asked Mikey if he had seen Eric, and he asked me why I wanted to know. I told him about finding Ropey's boat floating belly up on the far end of the lake, and that Eric was missing. Mike Niblin looked over at me. The faintest look of guilty realization crossed his face, and disappeared. "He's drowned then," was all Mikey said.

It turned out Mikey had heard that Ropey had gone to the Twin Cities. Mikey was out of everything he needed to take in order to keep things together. In desperation, he hitched a ride out to the beginning of the Gold Mine Road, and hiked in the rest of the way in to see if he could scrounge up anything from Eric. When Mikey found out all he could get from Eric was a pack of cigarettes, he started to get the heebie-jeebies. He asked if Eric would give him a ride back to town. The only thing Eric had available was the small twelve-foot boat, and Eric agreed to take Mikey to town in the boat.

The sun was nearing the western horizon when they headed southeast from the shelter of Boulder Bay. Things may not have been too bad on the two-mile ride over to Rolando's dock on the south side of the lake. They were going with the wind on the ride over, and Eric had Mike Niblin in the front of the boat to provide badly needed ballast, all which would have helped him in the big water. People on the lake that day told us the waves were over three feet, and were driven by a powerful and erratic northwest wind, with gusts closing in on fifty miles an hour. An experienced man would have picked up some rocks to put in the front of the boat for the ride back against the wind, but Eric from Toledo hadn't paid attention to little things like weighing down the front of the boat. Shaefer Bay is protected from such a wind by Brisson's Point, which runs due north from the lake's south shore. At the end of the point sits August the Great's Island, which is about forty feet off the end of the point. When any boat gets there, the wind hits you from two directions at the same time. The wind splits around the island and one wind bends hard to the east and runs up the point. The other wind comes from the other side of the island, and it can be a fatal combination if you aren't ready for it. That's where they figure the boat rolled over.

The only person who saw anything close to being conclusive was someone looking out their window, watching the sunset over the lake. This person lived close to where Ropey's dad had his place, about a quarter mile east of Shaefer Bay.

When he heard what had happened, he called Joe and told him that he spotted some movement out on the lake yesterday evening, just before dark. The fellow told Joe he went into the other room to pick up his binoculars, and when he came back, he spotted what must have been Ropey's capsized boat. Eric had already slipped beneath the waves. The man said in the fading light, the capsized boat looked like a duck sitting on a log. What the neighbor thought was a duck was probably the motor sticking up from the stern of the boat.

I brought Mike Niblin over to my house to face the music and to tell Ropey what he was doing over at the shack after he had been kicked out a few days before. With absolutely no remorse, Mikey told why he was out to the shack. Ropey told him in a very hard way that Eric's blood was on his head. After he had gone on for a while, I looked at Mikey, who was sitting near my kids. The kids were watching Punky Brewster on television. When Ropey started to repeat himself a second time, I told him he had said all that needed to be said, and he lapsed into a surly silence. Mikey Niblin turned to me, smiled a stupid smile, and told me that Punky Brewster was some kind of funny. He hadn't heard a word Ropey had said, or if he had, it rolled through his head and out his other ear without having made any impression. At that moment I knew that whatever Mike Niblin would end up doing with his life, being tormented by conscience wouldn't be a problem.

They fished Eric from Toledo out of the lake later that day, and I thought about the beautiful afternoon a few weeks back when we were eating turtle. I'd told Eric to be mindful of just how dangerous a lake can be in a big wind, and it felt ironic to think of him dead. Even though I really never liked the guy, I sat down one day and wrote to his mother in Toledo to tell her what had happened to her son. I thought it important for her to know what he had been doing the last few weeks of his life. I wanted to tell her that Eric had died in a beautiful place, living an adventure he had dreamed about for a long time.

Later that afternoon I stopped up at the sheriff's office, and asked the sheriff on duty if he could help me by giving me an address where I could mail my letter.

A cold look crossed his face. "What the hell you want to send that son of a bitch's mother a letter for? The world is better off, now that he drowned."

I came back with a terse response. "Isn't that being a little hard on a dead man's mother?"

"That man went into a liquor store in Toledo and pointed a sawed-off shotgun at a man he knew and blew the face right off his head. That's not anyone I want to write a letter for."

"It isn't for him I wrote the letter," I said. "It's for his mother."

He wrote the address on a piece of paper and slid it over to me without another word. I wrote the address on my letter, left the sheriff's office, walked a block to the post office, and mailed a letter to a woman I knew I would likely never meet.

On the way out to Ropey's, I thought about that long-ago morning when I met Eric coming down the road with the twelve-gauge shotgun, and I thought how lucky I was not to have pushed the issue with him of hunting grouse in the spring. I thought about those dark hawk-like eyes, which had nothing of warmth and compassion in them, and I felt lucky to be alive. There was no doubt in my mind he had done just what the sheriff told me. You can tell a lot of things about a person when you look into their eyes, and it was almost as if I could see the killer hiding behind them. Maybe that's why I never liked him; it was an instinct sort of a thing.

There was anger growing in me since I found out that Ropey had been living with a murderer. When I got into the cabin, Ropey was sitting at the table enjoying a cup of coffee. I asked him if he knew he had been harboring a killer.

"Well," Ropey replied, "we were sitting around the shack with Mike Niblin one night playing the 'what's the worst thing you ever did in your life game', and Eric told us that he had killed a guy in Toledo, but we thought he was just kidding."

I had never heard of the "What's the Worst Thing You Ever Did in Your Life Game" before, and I asked him if that was something he did often. I was relieved to hear that was the only time he ever did anything like that.

"Have you looked into his pack sack yet? "I asked.

"No I haven't."

We walked over toward Eric's bunk and pulled out a green canvas Duluth pack from the far side of the bunk. Ropey started pulling out clothes and other personal items, and started putting them on the bed. Most of the contents were out of the pack, when right at the bottom of the pack sat the mean looking sawed-off shotgun that had done such terrible business.

"Holy shit," said Ropey. "What the hell am I going to do now?"

"You're going to take that thing and you're going to throw it into the deepest part of the lake, and then you're going to take his stuff into town and give it to the sheriff."

Which was just what he did.

That was the last time we heard anything official about the matter, and I don't often think of Eric. But every time a big northwest wind blows through, I go down and watch the white-caps run down the fetch of Shagawa Lake. I think back to the spring when the lake took justice into her own hands and settled accounts with Eric from Toledo.

The Last Canoe Trip

When I came back across the Sheridan portage for my second load, he was standing at the end of the portage looking out over That Man Lake. Of all the lakes in the canoe country my dad loved the Man chain best. We never much went past the second and smallest of the four lakes, No Man, because the fishing was so good, and the time he had on the weekends made getting back into This Man and the Other Man something that time and distance didn't allow. The last two lakes in the chain were saved for vacations and long weekends, so most of the time he had with his partners Joe and Johnny was spent on That Man and No Man.

The old man and his partners were part of a tradition where the canoe country was parceled up between the local men. It was an unwritten code where everybody staked out a favorite part of the country based on respect and common sense. First, it gave everybody a feeling of space and freedom that later would be called wilderness. The second thing it did was spread everyone out over the country, which made it better for the country, because it evened out the demand.

I still remember the day when a canoe crossed over from Knife Lake, which lay south of the Man Chain. My dad turned to his partner Joe and said, "Why it's the Popishes. I wonder what the hell they are doing on our lake?" They waited until the canoe made its way over to where we were fishing, and before anyone else could say another word, Tony Popish yelled out that he was sorry to have to intrude on their space, but that it was too windy to fish on Knife Lake. The Popishes had their cousin Bernie with them, and when they said that Bernie had just been ordained a priest, Dad sort of growled an ok. But he also said not to make a habit of it. The Popishes thanked everyone for their hospitality, and then they headed towards the other end of the lake to show their respect by giving us as much space as possible.

By the time I started making regular trips with Dad and Joe in the 1960s, that system of managing the land had been in place for as long as anyone could remember, and there was no need for anyone to interfere. The people who traveled the country had a great understanding of the Quetico-Superior and, in most cases, lavished it with respect. I remember a summer evening when the fish were almost biting on a bare hook. I never wanted to stop. Then my dad said, "Mikey, you want to come back here again, don't you?" I answered that I always wanted to come back here.

Then he looked over at me and said, "Mikey, if we take all the fish out of the lake tonight there won't be any point in coming back again, will there? Maybe we should leave some for the next time." That was the simple lesson that was taught. You wanted to take care of the country, because you wanted to come back again.

I remember the first time we found someone had built a table and bench in one of our camps. Joe and the old man were hot about it. When I asked Dad what he was so mad about, he said that if anyone wanted to go on a picnic they should stay in a park or campground. The canoe county was no place for tables or benches.

It's hard just to say when things started to change. Maybe finding the tables and chairs started it. There was a time when everything was left in camp. Open the tent doors in case any bear would come nosing around, tie the food pack up in a tree, and camp was all set for when you came back next weekend. Then one Friday evening we pulled into camp and found a note pinned to the food pack with some change left on the flat rock that made such a good cooking table. "Borrowed some sugar and powdered milk," it read, "Thanks." After that, Dad and his partners started to break camp. Then there was the trip we came and found that someone had taken the spare canoe that was left hidden in the woods at the far end of the portage. Crime had come to the canoe country.

In order to understand the last trip my dad and I made, you have to understand the next-to-the-last trip. It was back in May of 1968, the year everything went crazy. Bill Rom made the front cover of *Argosy* magazine and the title proclaimed him "Canoe King." You might say it helped let the cat out of the bag regarding the canoe country of Northern Minnesota. When people found out how cheap it was to rent a canoe and camping gear, and that there were virtually no rules about where you could camp or how long you could stay, they descended en masse. It was Memorial Day weekend, and we were traveling with Don Berg, one of Dad's friends from the mine. The trip up wasn't bad until we got to the portage going from Carp Lake to That Man, and you could see where someone had taken out a number of trees along the portage in order to make it wider. "I wonder what the hell is going on?" the old man said. It was the same with the next portage.

The answer to the riddle came on No Man's Lake when we saw two sixteen-foot boats pulled up along the shore of what used to be our camp, but was now in the domain of what Dad referred to with scorn as "fish hogs." When we pulled close to camp you could see trout hanging all around camp, dozens of them.

"Fishing looks to be pretty good," Dad said to the men who had come down to see what was up.

"Yeah," one of them answered, "It's been great, and we've only just started."

I remember the look on my father's face as we pulled away from that camp. It was as if he had seen the thing he loved best destroyed right in front of his eyes, and you could read the hurt on his face. "I can't stay here," he said to Don Berg, "I've just got to get out of here." Don Berg shook his head and pointed the canoe back towards the portage.

When we came back for the second load the old man walked into the woods around the end of the portage, and in a short time came back carrying a set of portage wheels, which he proceeded to heave out into the lake. "Those bastards are going to have a harder time getting those boats back out than they did coming in," he said. Then he picked up the last pack and, without a backward glance, walked down the portage. On the way back home we counted over three hundred canoes heading into the country, along with a score of boats. My father never said a word all the way back.

Dad had many chances to go back into the country. He used to tell people that the portages were getting longer and steeper and that he no longer had enough steam in his boiler to make it over the rim of the Canadian Shield. Although we never talked about it, I always knew that the reason was the things he had seen on that trip. He had seen the best of it, and now he had seen the worst of it, and he wanted to remember it the way it had always been.

In 1987 I was back running my old canoe base on Moose Lake. Dad and Mom would stop out at least once a week to say hello and to allow Dad to do some fishing off the dock. One day I had to take some fishing equipment up to a party who had left it sitting on the shore of the landing, and I asked my dad if he wanted to take a ride to the Ranger Station at Prairie Portage. At first he said no, but when I pressed him by telling him that things had gotten a lot better since 1968, he reluctantly agreed. On the way up the three lake chain to Prairie Portage we passed seven canoes with our tow boat, and the old man told me that this was more like it.

When we got to the portage, we were informed by the ranger that the head of Quetico Park was paying a visit, and we had best make sure that everything was in order. By a twist of fate, the head of the park ended up being an old friend of my father's whom Dad had met when Don Money was a young ranger back in the 1950s. They had a wonderful visit talking about the old days and the way things used to be. On the way back the he turned to me and said that maybe they had turned things around and that he'd like to see more of it.

That next spring, Dad and I took our final trip to No Man's Lake. The trees of our old camp had filled back in, and we fell asleep at night listening to the sound of the river heading north. It was like being home again, and was a wonderful trip. Everyone caught fish, except Dad, but he didn't seem to care; he was past that point in his life. All we saw were two canoes that passed through our near perfect wilderness, like a mirage, and were gone.

Dad was standing at the end of the portage when I came up to him and asked him if he was coming, or if he planned to come home with someone else.

"I want to thank you for bringing me back here," he said. "This is the last time I'm ever going to see this lake and I wanted to thank you for the gift."

"Don't be going soft and mushy on me," I said.

"No," he answered, "It's just that I'm no damned good any more, got no sense of balance, can't carry a pack any more, it's time for me to call it quits. This is a place for young people and not for old farts like me. But I want to thank you for giving me back something I'd lost. This is the way it was before, and this is the way it should always be, and now, thanks to this trip, it's the way I will always remember it." Then he turned back to the lake.

I picked up the last pack and headed toward Sheridan Lake and the way back home. Whenever I think of my father, he is standing at the end of that portage, looking east into the rising sun shining down on the place he loved the best.

The Old Shovel

A good snow shovel doesn't get to be a prized personal possession much these days. It's rarely considered a special tool. Although you might not enjoy using it, you might admire the quality of its craft and construction. I think indifference to shovels occurs today because most people don't shovel snow any more. They have purchased a snow blower and relegated the old shovel to porch duty or a permanent place out in the garage. Or, having reached a certain point of financial security along with a particular level of winter weariness, they pay other people to clear their walks and driveways. But a few old dinosaurs such as me still find some attachment to that old snow shovel.

Today most shovels are store-bought and many of them have shiny, neon-colored blades, carbon fire technology, and scientifically bent handles that are supposed to make shoveling less stressful on your back. My wife prefers one of those shovels, and I always say it shows a lot of thoughtfulness when a man thinks enough of his wife to make sure she has the latest, state-of-the-art snow shovel at her disposal. I personally like to use my dad's old shovel. It is a homemade shovel that has been in the family for over fifty years, and has moved a lot of snow. Not that Dad had sole rights to the shovel. Say what you will about my father, but being selfish with his handmade snow shovel was not one of his faults. As a matter of fact, it was my mom who did most of the shoveling that was done with Dad's shovel.

It was called Dad's shovel because it was made especially for my dad by John Skule Sr., the blacksmith at the Zenith Mine. My dad used to make beautiful knives from worn out files and hacksaw blades. A neighbor kid, Johnny Skule, grandson of the blacksmith at the mine, wanted one of my dad's knives in the worst way. One Christmas, a trapper who had ordered a knife didn't show to pick it up. My dad took it, crossed the alley to Skule's, and gave the knife to young Johnny Skule right in front of his beaming grandfather.

After that Christmas my father could do no wrong in the eyes of Grandpa Skule. "Checker," the old man would say with a deep Slavic accent. "You want chisel? You want shovel? Anything you want I geeeve to you." That's how Dad acquired our snow shovel. John Skule made it for him in the Zenith Mine blacksmith shop and you can still see the initials Z. M. welded on the blade of the shovel. That was supposed to keep the shovels close to the mine. It didn't work.

My dad was one of the tool men at the Zenith Mine. Mining was tough on men and equipment. Things like picks and axes were always getting dull, and guys were always breaking shovel handles. In many cases the breakage was intentional. My dad said there were just some men who couldn't have enough shovels, so to smuggle the blade past security guards, they would cut it off near the base of the handle, and then slip the blade under their coveralls. Once my dad had to call Ben Richards, the mine superintendent, to tell him that all of the one hundred fifty spades that were in the tool room last week were gone. After a thoughtful pause, Ben Richards' response to my father was, "My, my, Chester. You'd think that every man in Ely would have at least two shovels by now."

I admired my father today as I cleared the wet heavy snow from the front walk. Not for his snow moving capability, which was not one of his strong suits. I think Dad figured that a man only had so much snow to move in his life, and he preferred to save his shoveling for digging out a place for his portable fishing shelter, preferably out on a trout lake. What I admired about him was the intuition that told him that people like my mother and her father were compulsive snow shovelers. They couldn't stand to see a sidewalk covered with even half an inch of snow, and they couldn't resist having at a good snowfall. My father knew the simple compulsive truth; that if you left a quality snow shovel in a conspicuous spot, someone from the other side of the family couldn't help but use it.

Heck, I even remember my grandfather, Steve Thompson, waking me up before dawn so that we could clear our sidewalk and then move over to the Presbyterian Church, where he was the janitor, to do that walkway as well. Grandpa never had to take the shovel from our house because he had worked at the Pioneer Mine, so he had his own shovel at the church with the letters PM emblazoned on the blade. I remember asking him why we were shoveling snow in the dark. The old man looked up from his work and said that when God's day began, Steve Thompson's sidewalks would be ready for the morning. Like I say, that side of the family was compulsive about their snow shoveling.

Since its creation over fifty years ago, the old shovel has served four generations of our family. When I think of my father, and his special relationship to that old shovel, the one sad thing for me is that neither my son or daughter have that old Thompson compulsion for snow shoveling.

The Last Song for Bernice

Sometimes fate takes a hand in your life, and you end up being in the right place at exactly the time you need to be there. That's why when I look back to that long-ago Sunday morning, and remember the last time I talked to my old friend Bernice Paulson, it seems to me that I was meant to be there. Bernice was always one of my favorite people. She lived across the street from us, and our families got to know each other well. My dad and Bernice's husband Lynn had gone on quite a few fishing trips together, and Mom and Bernice were close friends. We were members of the Presbyterian Church where Mrs. Paulson and my mom taught Sunday school. Bernice Paulson was a special person in many ways, and because of all her hard work, and dedication, she was the first woman elder elected to serve in the history of our church.

What made the two of us especially close was that I was born with a good singing voice, and Mrs. Paulson's pride and joy was directing her Junior Church Choir. Laurie Langen accompanied the Junior Choir and played the church hymns. I can't quite remember how many years I sang for Bernice, but much of the joy I have about making music goes back to the days of singing in the junior choir. One of the things I remember best about my choirboy days is singing for the Christmas Eve church service. We all wore matching half-length choir robes that our mothers had bleached as white as Christmas snow. Everyone was scrubbed shiny for the occasion. A hurricane could not have moved a hair on my head from the amount of hair tonic Mother used in order to subdue my cowlicks and keep them from popping up during the service. The local Boy Scout troop made candle holders out of split birch logs, which lined the windows of the sanctuary and gave the church a warm golden glow.

Mrs. Paulson had purchased battery-operated candles for everyone in the choir, to add to the beauty of the occasion. In an effort to have them blend in, they were made of metal that had been painted the same light green of the church sanctuary walls. It was long before computers, and we all thought those green battery-operated candle holders with a screw in bulb, which was meant to look like a flame, were the neatest things in the world. We weren't supposed to turn them on until we marched from the back of the sanctuary and up to the choir loft, but everyone had to check to make sure their candle was working. There wasn't a Christmas Eve where someone either screwed their bulb in too tight and ended up holding the top of a cracked bulb with the metal base still in the candle holder, or someone's batteries ran out of juice at just the wrong time. But Mrs. Paulson was prepared for any emergency. She always carried a handkerchief to dry the tears of some luckless and lightless soul. Bernice always hauled around a huge purse loaded with extra bulbs and batteries, which had been supplied by her husband's hardware store *gratis*.

Even though it has been many years since my junior choir days, I can still remember our old warm-up song, complete with gestures:

>*Send Your Tones Straight Fourth Like Arrows*
>*Sing For the Man Next Door To Admire*
>*Use Your Head and Watch Your Leader*
>*Let's Be Proud Of The Junior Choir.*

I had not seen Bernice for a number of years when we met that Sunday morning, and it was good to see her again. She had lost her vision a few years earlier, and the last years of her life were lived in darkness, but it never extinguished the wonderful light that burned within her. Mother and I were sitting in our accustomed spot in the last pew on the left side of the church. The back pew was a privileged spot reserved for a number of older ladies who referred to themselves as the back pew gals, and they would remind me quite often how lucky I was to be included as part of their club. When I asked Mother why she preferred sitting in the back of the church, she told me it was import to see who was in attendance, and even more important to see who wasn't.

I was especially fond of Mother's friend Elma who was hard of hearing. Elma loved to say asides to the ladies sitting next to her. They were supposed to be close-kept secrets, but Elma was so deaf her remarks were clearly heard by anyone around her. Once we were at a funeral service and the minister was praising the newly departed. Elma put her bulletin up to her face and asked Mother if the minister was speaking about the person whose name was printed in the bulletin, or one of the saints of heaven. There never seemed to be a dull moment for the back pew gals.

Mrs. Paulson and her daughter Lynnese were sitting in the pew in front of us that morning, and we had a wonderful time visiting before service. During worship I enjoyed seeing that even though she was blind, Bernice still enjoyed singing. In order to bolster her courage and keep her faith, Bernice purchased collections of almost every hymn you could think of, and had committed most of them to memory.

Like everyone else, Bernice had seen her share of sorrows. One of the finest memories I have of her is when she stood up in front of the church at her son Nick's funeral. Knowing how people like to gossip, and not wanting that to happen, Bernice told the church that she wanted everyone to know that although she didn't understand why, Nick had taken his own life and she wanted everyone to know the truth. It was one of the most courageous things I ever saw.

The last hymn of the service that Sunday was "Amazing Grace," and we were all singing away to the best of our various abilities. What Mrs. Paulson wasn't aware of was that in order to be more socially correct, the last line of the hymn had been changed in the new hymnals, but not in her collection of hymns that still had the original words. When we got to the last line of "Amazing Grace," the only person in church who wasn't aware of the change was Bernice Paulson, so of course when we reached the final stanza, she stuck out like a sore thumb. I still smile when I hear her saying, "Damn, I hate it when they do that. Why can't they just leave well enough alone!" It was one of the most charming moments I had seen, and that's when fate seemed to take a hand.

I don't know why but I asked her what her favorite hymn was, and she asked me why I wanted to know. I told her that maybe if I knew what it was, I would sing it at her funeral. Her daughter Lynnese turned and said, "Mother isn't going to have a funeral." Bernice responded by saying that maybe if she knew that Michael Hillman was going to sing at the service, maybe she would change her mind and have one. She told me her favorite hymns were "When I Survey the Wondrous Cross" and the old Welsh song "All Through the Night."

I asked her why she liked the second song so much, and she told me when she was a little girl her father worked as a Captain in one of the underground mines. Bernice overheard her mom and dad talking about how dangerous the work was. Sometimes she would wake up in the night feeling scared for her father, and whenever that happened he would come into her room to offer comfort. The last thing her father would do before he tucked her back into bed was to sit her on his lap and sing "All Through the Night."

I told my old friend that she had a deal and I would see to it that both songs would be included in her service, which I thought would be years in the future. The last thing I did before we hugged and said goodbye was to sing our old warm-up song. I can still see the smile that crossed her face when she knew that I still remembered the song after all those years.

Three days later I received a phone call from Mrs. Paulson's daughter Lynnese telling me that her mother had passed away earlier that day. Five days later I fulfilled my promise to my old friend, by singing at her funeral.

    I have lived most of my life thinking we're on our own in this world, because God has a universe to run. We should help out by taking care of our own lives as best we can. But there are times such as that long-ago Sunday morning when it seemed that fate took me by the hand and placed me right where I needed to be. Singing those two songs meant much, because I was able to give back part of the gift a good friend gave to me when I was a little boy. Whenever I hear "Amazing Grace" and get to the final verse of the hymn, I smile and say a prayer to the memory of an old friend.

The Mad Miner
Or
The Tragic Tale of Pick 'Em to Death Pete Peterson

I was his friend before any of this mad miner business started. No one who knew Pete Peterson would have guessed things would turn out the way they did. The first thing you noticed about him was just how damned big he was. Pete stood a good six foot six and the last time he fought for the heavy weight championship of the Lone Pine Mine, he weighed in at two hundred fifty-five pounds. He could have made a fine professional boxer if he had any of the killer instinct, but a granite jaw would only carry you so far. Pete Peterson was the living definition of the term "gentle giant." For all the world there didn't seem to be a mean bone in that great big body, but then Anna Anders came to town, and everything started to change.

Anna Anders was one of the most beautiful women I had ever seen; tall and thin, who moved with the fluid beauty of a dancer. Her face was like a winter sunrise, all alabaster and gold. Like many adventurous young women, she had opted to leave home in order see what kind of a life she could build for herself in America. When Anna read about jobs in Minnesota, she wrote to Mr. and Mrs. Thompson, who ran a boarding house in town. She told of her interest in working off her passage as a maid at their house.

In the early days there weren't enough houses for all the

men who came to work in the mines. People with enough money in their poke put up a boarding house to take advantage of all those single men who needed a place to hang their hat at the end of the day. You didn't rent a room in those days. You and another fella who had good manners and took a bath at least once a week, like any decent human being, would rent out a bed in a room not much bigger than a closet. When we would head down to the mine for our shift, they would rent the bed out to two other guys on the opposite shift, in order to maximize their investment.

The only day that was a real problem was Sunday when the mine shut down. Things got mighty crowded on Sundays. They would feed the men two meals a day, and if any miner wanted a hot meal delivered when they brought the men up for lunch, one of the girls would run the meal down to the mine.

That's where we first saw Anna Anders. She had just come into town on the morning train, and two of the men, who had signed up for one of Mrs. Thompson's wonderful lunches, were Pete Peterson and I. We had just come back to grass after spending five hours working by candlelight, and we were still squinting our way back to adjusting to the bright sunlight. We were looking down the path expecting to see Hanna Hendrickson coming through the cow pasture that separated the mine from the Captain's house when we saw this beautiful girl break into a run when one of the cows started to chase her. We found out later she was afraid of cows, and when we opened our lunch buckets, most of the coffee that rested at the bottom of the bucket had spilled all over the sandwiches, doughnuts, and generous slice of apple pie. I remember looking at Pete Peterson, and he had a look on his face that told me as clear as if it was written on his forehead, that he was in love. When Anna started to apologize for the soggy state of our lunches, all Pete said was that we would have probably dunked everything anyway, and that she shouldn't worry about it.

I don't think anyone can understand just how lonesome a man can get for the company of a good woman unless you lived in mining town where good women were at a premium.

The only pleasant company available to most men was at the bawdy houses such as Daisy Redfield's or Nell McCarty's where many a lonely man found comfort in the arms of one of the fallen angels. But most of the men were looking for something better, and it was really when the boarding houses started up that a whole new kind of woman was available to men who were looking for something more than the company of whores. When a man spends six days a week, ten hours a day, by the light of a beeswax candle, looking at the back side of a mule, mining iron with other rust-stained men working in the wet and dangerous darkness, it is amazing how good some average-looking women get to be.

It didn't take long before the boarding houses all had contracts with their girls that stated they would work until their passage was paid in full, and many a miner paid off contracts so that they could get married and start a decent life. If an average woman looked that good, you can imagine what a stir someone like Anna Anders caused, and before the week was out every Swede and Norwegian in town was out to win her hand. That's when I first saw the demon that lurked in the shadows inside Pete Peterson.

The only real rival Pete Peterson faced in winning Anna's hand was Large Lars Larson, the very man that Pete had beaten the year before in the heavyweight boxing championship bout. There was bad blood between those two, and everyone in town was wondering when it was going to go from a strong simmer to the boiling point, but they didn't have to wait long. Rumor has it that one day after work when the men were making their way back to town, Pete Peterson told Large Lars that he wouldn't allow him to continue his courtship of Miss Anna. Larson responded by telling Peterson to mind his own business, and that Pete could kiss his ass. That's when it all broke loose.

At first Large Lars held his own, but he was used to a big gentle giant who was always afraid of hurting someone, and he wasn't prepared to deal with a man driven crazy by jealousy. The only thing that saved Lars Larson was that Father Buh happened to be driving by and he stopped the fight. It was weeks before Larson was back at work, and by that time, Anna Anders had become Mrs. Pete Peterson. Larson swore an oath to himself that he would find a way to get even with Pete Peterson.

I don't know if there was a lot of happiness for Anna Anders in the short time she and Pete were married. Jealousy is a terrible thing that eats away at some people until they just don't see things straight any more. One night some poor fool, who was new to town and didn't understand what he was doing, asked her to dance. It was the first and last time anyone asked her to dance ever again. The stranger looked as if he had been kicked by a mule the next morning when he headed out of town on the first train. After that Anna Peterson saw one fun thing after another taken from her, until about all that was left to her was church on Sunday, and the hope of a wedding or funeral to break the dull monotony of her days.

One snowy winter night when the men were sitting in the Miners Dry House eating their lunches, Lars Larson looked down to the other end of the dry (changing house) to where Pete Peterson sat alone eating lunch. He turned to his partners and he asked if they would care to help him play a little joke on Pete Peterson. When Otto Harri asked what it was, Larson told them of a plan that had been cooking on the back burner ever since the day after the big fight.

"All you have to do is finish lunch early, and walk down to Peterson's house. When you get there I want you to walk up to the back steps and then walk out backwards in the same steps," said Larson. "Then I want you to get down there again right at the end of the shift, and I want you to walk in backwards to the front steps of the house. Then you walk back out in the same tracks you came in on."

"What do I want to do that for?" asked Otto Harri.

"I want that son of a bitch to think that his beautiful little princess has found a new prince. Let her see him for what he really is," answered the vengeful Swede.

Otto Harri did just as he was told, and as the two other men who worked the contract with them we getting ready to head home for a good day's rest, Lars Larson asked them to join him for some free drinks in honor of the joke. On their way down to the Arcade Saloon, they passed the Peterson house, where a set of footprints was clearly visible in the snow.

Like many men who work hard enough to hurt at the end of the shift, it was my custom to head down to the Arcade for two shots of whiskey, and a couple of beers to chase them down. When I came into the Arcade, the four men who made up what was referred to as the Larson contract were in the process of slamming them down with a vengeance. When he saw me, Large Lars couldn't wait to come over to share what he and the boys had done to finally get even with Pete Peterson.

The blood left my face, and I sat there like a duck that had been hit on the head. I was stunned. It took me some time before I was able to muster myself into action. I looked over at him and said, "Larson you're a goddamned fool, and if anything happens to that poor girl, it's all going to be on your stupid head." Then I headed out the door as fast as I could to the Peterson house, hoping I would be in time to spare them both an ugly scene.

I was breathing hard when I got to the house, and as I made my way up the walk, I could hear Pete Peterson angrily asking his wife who it was that she was sharing her bed with. I heard Anna swear to him that there was no one but him. As I came through the door I heard him say, "Don't compound your sin by telling me a lie, tell me who it is," as he gave her a shake like some rag doll.

I know he didn't mean to hurt her, but you could hear her neck break even from the far side of the room. As I watched her go limp in his arms a sigh came up out of somewhere deep in me.

"You poor fool," I said. "There wasn't never anyone here last night, or any night for that matter. You been set up by Lars Larson and the boys he works with. Larson wanted to pay you back ever since you put that hurting on him, so he had Otto Harri put them tracks coming in the back yard during last night's lunch hour, and then he had him do the front tracks right at the end of the shift. He wanted her to see you for what you really are, and now look what you done."

He stood there stunned for a long while, and then he looked down at his beautiful Anna hanging limp in his arms. He reached down and touched her face, and then he shook her gently and said, "Anna, are you all right? I am so sorry if I hurt you. That was never my intent."

But she wasn't all right; she was dead. I heard a sound come out of the deep part of him that I will never be able to forget. It started out as a low groan that was nothing but pure grief, but then it changed to a growl that had nothing in it but pure hate. He picked her up and brought her into the parlor where he laid her down on the sofa and then he turned to me.

I thought I was going to die that day, but all he said was that I was to head down to Doc Shipman's to see if there was something he could do for Anna. I told him I would go there as fast as I could. Then he moved past me and out the door. As he moved down the sidewalk he came to the place where the pick and shovel stood that he used to clear the walk way, he grabbed the pick, and headed toward a date with destiny at the Arcade Saloon.

I knew there was no good going to come out of this day, so I started off as fast as I could towards the police station, to see if we couldn't stop him from doing what I knew he was going to do. When I got to the station I was breathing hard, and it took all I could do to suck in enough wind to tell Charlie Smith, the officer on duty, just what was going on. Charlie's boy Billy was down at the station, and the first thing Charlie did was to get over to Harvey Street to let Chief Vail know what was going on down at the Arcade, and to have him meet us there. Charlie turned to me and said that I was officially sworn in as a deputy, and that I should grab a gun and follow him.

It was all over by the time when we got to the Arcade. The place looked like a bomb had gone off. Tables and chairs had been smashed to pieces and two men lay on the floor in a huge pool of blood, beer, and spilled whiskey. Tom Harris lay face up with glazed eyes staring sightlessly up at the kerosene lamps that hung from the ceiling. Charlie Smith turned the second man over, and there was Ned Turner with a now-dead face frozen in fear.

"Don't know if Tom Harris knew what hit him," said Charlie Smith, "but I know damn well that Ned Turner could see the elephant coming." The chief came busting through the doors, service pistol drawn ready for serious business.

From the accounts of those who witnessed what happened, the one thing everyone agreed on was that everything happened fast. They said that before anyone knew it, Pete Peterson had burst through the doors of the Arcade like a bull moose in rut. The bartender yelled that you couldn't be bringing a pick into the Arcade Saloon. Just as the bartender reached for the short shotgun that was kept beneath the bar for just such occasions, Pete Peterson grabbed the bartender by the hair, and slammed his face into the bar, knocking him colder than a mackerel.

Lars Larson and Otto Harri were facing the door, and they started to move as soon as they saw what was coming at them. Tom Harris turned just in time to receive a blow from that terrible pick that caught him square in the heart. He was dead before he hit the floor. Ned Turner was able to take three steps towards his two friends heading out the door before the first blow caught him just below the left shoulder. But Ned Turner was quick on his feet. He managed to evade several vicious swings before he stumbled over a spittoon, and death finally caught up with Ned Turner.

By this time a large group of people had gathered around, and Chief Vail told all the men there who had guns to go home and get them, and to meet back at the Arcade in five minutes.

Faster than you could whistle Yankee Doodle, a large group of citizens was following Chief Vale and his entire three-man force up the hill towards the Lone Pine Mine.

"Hope those two are good runners," Chief Vail said to Charlie Smith as they headed up the hill towards the Head-Frame of Lone Pine Mine, which was the town's dominant feature. About halfway to the mine, they came upon a group of people who were looking down at the body of Otto Harri, whose body was filled with wounds. There was a trail of blood from where the first blow had fallen, to the spot where he finally lay, and you could see that Otto Harri had died hard.

"Come on," said the chief to no one in particular. "There ain't anything any of us can do for him other than to get him down to the undertakers, so why don't some of you men get him down there, and tell Father Buh to get over to offer some comfort to Mrs. Harri."

With that done, the mob of people, which had grown considerably by this time, headed off towards the head frame of the mine to see what had happened between Large Lars and Peterson. That was the first time I ever heard the name Pick 'Em to Death Pete. Don't recall as to who said it first, but before you knew it everyone in the crowd seemed to be shouting it, as more and more people joined in the excitement.

When the throng of people reached the head frame, a few men were standing at the shaft, talking about how Lars Larson had come up the hill looking like the devil himself was close behind. They said that Larson didn't say a word, and before they knew it, he grabbed a few candles, climbed down the ladder, and disappeared in the darkness. A minute or two later, a blood-soaked Peterson burst on the scene with a wild look in his eyes. He asked where Larson was and they told him that he had gone down into the mine. They said he grabbed the hat off one of the men, picked up a handful of candles, and followed Larson down in the dark.

There was nobody that ever expected to see Larson alive again, and it was a big surprise when he came up one of the vent shafts several hours later. He had hidden away in one of the abandoned areas of the mine and when Peterson continued past him down the ladder to the lower levels, Larson held his breath and waited in the dark until he was sure the danger was past. Then without even risking a light, he climbed back up one of the vent shafts until he was back on the surface. The few people who saw him said that he was as white as a sheet, and that as he ran he kept looking back over his shoulder, and mumbling to himself about getting out of town. The last anyone saw of Lars Larson was when he climbed aboard the afternoon train. When the conductor asked him where he was headed, all he said was as far away from here as possible, and then he was gone.

A few of the women from the church had gone over to the Peterson House. They picked out a beautiful white dress trimmed with spring green that Anna had worn for Easter Sunday. They brought it down to the Lainge Funeral Parlor where she was laid out in a casket that had been paid for by the Thompsons, who had learned to love her like a daughter. Those that saw her said she was as beautiful in death as she had been in life, and she looked as if she was only asleep and would wake from her slumber. Plans were made for a funeral that would take place that next afternoon, and soon Anna Anders Peterson was left alone in the quiet dark.

When Mr. Lainge came to work the next morning he found an empty casket. Someone had taken her body. There were some who wondered who could have done something like that. But I knew who had done it, and I knew where she would be. I was positive she would be down in the mine with the man that loved her even unto death. That night, after the town had gone to sleep, Pete Peterson had left the mine, and gone to the mortuary and taken her body.

"We should have never left her alone," said one of the deputies.

"How in the hell was anyone to know that he would take her body?" replied the chief.

Captain Hall burst through the door and told the chief that someone had broken in the storehouse at the mine. When they took stock of what had been stolen, they found dozens of candles and several boxes of dynamite missing.

"Now who in the hell do you figure would steal dynamite and candles?" asked an exasperated chief.

"I think you'll find them down in the crystal cavern," I said. The crystal cavern was one of the most beautiful places that anyone could imagine. Nobody knew for sure just why that cave had formed underground, but over the course of millions of years, the cavern had filled with the most beautiful crystals that anyone could imagine. Hard-bitten Cousin Jacks, who had seen everything you could imagine in an underground mine, made special trips to the cave just to see it glitter.

"Captain Hall, would you mind leading me and my deputies down to that place so we can settle this business once and for all?" asked the chief.

"Don't think that would be the thing to do," replied Captain Hall. Then he turned to me and said, "Bill, you know Peterson as well as anyone, and if there's any reason left in the man, you're the person to find it. Would you be willing to give it a chance?"

Thinking about going down in the mine to talk to a man crazed with grief left me with a cold feeling in the pit of my stomach, but I swallowed hard, and shook my head yes.

Going down into that mine was the hardest thing I ever did, but whatever you might have said to me about Pete Peterson, he had been a good friend that had once dug me out when a timber came down on me. I felt I owed him something. If nothing else, I wanted to see if I could persuade him to at least see that Anna was given a proper burial. The captain, chief, and deputies came down with me as far as the shaft station on level eleven, and I will always remember that quarter mile walk up to the place where I knew Pete Peterson would be waiting. As I got near the cave, I could see light glowing up ahead.

"Pete," I yelled, "It's me, Bill Eamons. I need to talk to you. I'm alone and unarmed, and I'd like to come in if I could."

If I live to be a hundred I'll never forget the sound of that voice telling me to come in, or the sight that greeted my eyes.

There were dozens of candles scattered around that cave, and there in the center of the glittering cavern lay Anna Peterson. She was laid out on a bier of dynamite boxes, looking beautiful in the candlelight that was reflected in crystals that gave out flashes of light, like moonlight shining on new snow.

Pete Peterson had been kneeling down in front of her makeshift bier, and as he got up to face me, I could see the tears streaming down his cheeks. As I looked around the cave, I could see that dynamite had been rigged around the entrance of the cavern.

"Why don't you let me get a supply cart, so I can take Anna back to grass. She can have a proper funeral, and then you can do whatever you think best."

The big man looked out from eyes that were red from grieving. "She don't need no one speaking a few words over her, and then putting her in the ground. Some things are too beautiful to put in the ground. I remember how much she liked them crystals that I brought her, and how she told me that someday she would like to see a place filled with such beauty. This is going to be her sepulcher where she is going to stay forever."

I stood there not knowing what to say and then I said, "If you don't want to have her leave, then at least let me bring Pastor Thorson down to make her right with God."

Then he laughed the saddest laugh I ever heard. "She's right with God even as we speak, and that's a place I'll never see, because there just ain't that much forgiveness in all the world. There's just one piece of business left for me to do, and as soon as I find that worthless son of a bitch who made me kill the thing I loved best in the world, is to kill him in as hard a way possible."

"That might be harder than you think, Pete. When Larson climbed out of the mine yesterday, the men that saw him said he looked as if death was hot on his trail, and the last anyone saw of him was him heading west on the first train out of town."

Then he walked back to where Anna was, and he knelt down, putting his big hand on her face. "I never meant to hurt you, Anna," he said with a sob. The he held his right hand up in the air, and swore on the soul of his dead wife that no matter how long it took, or wherever the trail led, that he wouldn't rest until he killed Lars Larson.

"Now it's time for you to go back, and tell them to stay

away, because once you leave, I'm going to seal this cave forever. But I wanted to thank you for your friendship and all that you tried to do for me and Anna."

Then he waved his hand at me, signaling me to head back the way I came. That was the last time I saw Pete Peterson. I can still see him standing there over the body of his Anna, surrounded by dozens of candles reflecting off the crystals. It was a long walk back to the shaft, and just as I reached the end of my walk. I heard the blast go off and felt the rush of air blow past me as the candle blew out and I stood there in the dark. Then I heard the cage start down the shaft, and soon I was in the company of the captain, and the chief who came out of the cage with his service pistol in hand.

"Boy, are we glad to see you, Bill. We thought you were a goner when we heard that blast go off. So tell us what's up with Pete Peterson."

Then I told them my story, and when the smoke started to clear, we headed back and found that the entrance to the crystal cave had been sealed by tons of rock. Captain Hall looked at the chief and asked if he wanted him to bring a crew of men to dig Anna out.

The chief didn't say anything for a while and then he said in a quiet voice, "No, I reckon she's in the place where she was meant to be, and I don't think we should disturb her any more."

"What about Peterson?" asked the chief. "Is there another way out of there?"

"The only way out would be through the old works, but they caved in years ago, and even if there was a way out, I don't think anyone could have survived that blast."

We walked back to the shaft and headed back to grass.

There were all kinds of rumors as far as what happened to Pete Peterson. Some of the men working close to the area of Anna Peterson's tomb swore that they heard the sound of a pick coming from the other side of the caved ground. Miners are a superstitious lot, and soon none of the men wanted to work in that part of the mine any more, so they left it to the dark. For years, old-timers would scare kids around town by telling them the story of Pick 'Em to Death Pete Peterson, the mad miner.

    I never held much to the stories that grew up around what exactly happened on the other side of that caved ground, but there were times when I wished we would have opened up that crystal cavern. I hadn't given a thought to Pete Peterson for years. One day a letter came in the mail with a newspaper clipping from a place in California about a man named Olson who was found brutally murdered. There was no apparent reason for the death, because he was found with a wallet filled with cash. The only shocking thing was the cause of death. The results of the autopsy revealed the weapon that killed Carl Olson was a pick.

The Old Settlers Journal

Excerpts from the Journal of Bill Trax

November 12, 1883. Norway, Michigan. The whole town is buzzing. One of the big mining men is coming to town to talk to Captain Morcomb about recruiting miners to move west to Minnesota. Louie Baribue's cousin Maurice gave up on mining here and moved west of Wisconsin to start a trap line. When I asked Louie why his cousin had moved, he told me his cousin told him things had become too crowded for him in the Upper Peninsula. Almost everything we came from Quebec for is gone. The trees are gone, the beaver is gone, the moose is gone. Everything is gone except the iron and soon that will be gone too. I admire Maurice. If it was not for Mary Ellen, I think I would have gone west with him looking for furs.

    Like me, Maurice did not like to go underground to mine iron. He did not do it, because he did not like climbing ladders. Me, I don't like it because I do not like closed places. But why do I still do it, I ask myself? I do it because it's all I know to do.

    Would I rather be on my grandfather's farm in Quebec? Yes, I would. If wishes were fishes I think many of us here would swim back to Montreal. But there were too many of us for Grandfather's farm to feed, which is why we crossed the water and came to work for the Yankees. Maurice came home to us here in Norway, because after traveling all that way thinking he would find nothing but Indians in the wilds of

Minnesota, he found a bunch of miners there.

Maurice told Louie he got to Duluth, and then traveled three days north to Lake Vermilion. When he got there he found a camp of fifty men trying to mine the iron. They asked him if he was one of the miners that Mr. Tower, who owned the mine, had hired to help them do what needed to be done. Maurice told them no. Then he came home. Maurice told us that he had seen it all before and that he was going to travel back home, and then head north of Quebec to the land of the Cree Indians where there was none of that going on. That is why I think the rumors are true about some big man coming to town looking for miners.

And what of me? What will I do? If given a chance, I will head west to Minnesota. My life is all ahead of me, but if I stay here, before I know it my life will all be behind me. In Minnesota it will always be before me. Time for us to follow the sun, I think.

November 25th 1883. We have a day off from work today, thanks to President Abraham Lincoln. I asked Mary Ellen if I should have voted for him, but she told me he is dead. Before he died he declared this day a national day of thanksgiving. Though he is dead, I would still vote for him. Because of him we don't have work today, and I can stay home with my family. I am thankful this day, because I have a beautiful wife to be thankful for, and I am thankful because I don't have to put a candle on my hat, and go down to work in the Vulcan Mine. It is much better, I think, to spend the day with my Mary Ellen, who is busy cooking even while I write these words.

Mary Ellen comes from Ireland, and she told me that on this day all good Americans are eating turkey. One of the men at work said we are really all eating crow, but Mary Ellen is going to school after supper in order to learn how to be a good American, and I think she knows best. I don't have time to go to school, so at night, at the supper table, I listen to her talk about just what a good American is, and how it differs from being a good Habitant. Mary Ellen told me that all good Americans are eating turkey today, because that is what they ate at the first Thanksgiving many years ago. When Mary Ellen told me what we should be eating, I dedicated that in my heart, but I did not succeed. It is the reason we are having ruffed grouse and goose on this day. In a way it is better I think, because now there is no fighting over the Pope's Nose. God did not choose turkeys to live here. Had he done that, we would be eating turkey today like Mister Lincoln and the pilgrims intended us to do, but I can only shoot what's here, and if nobody else understands why, I'm sure the Indians and Mr. Lincoln also know. A man just can't shoot what isn't there.

I am also thankful because I hear the rumors about some bigwig coming to town are true. They say his name is Edward Breitung, and he is coming to town next month looking for good men to work in a new mine in Minnesota. I believe I am just what he is looking for. I was talking to Charlie Nelson, the engineer at the Vulcan, and we were talking about going or staying in Norway. Charlie is about twenty years older than me, and he told me that he is staying in Norway. He figures there is about ten more years of iron here, and that will take him as far as he needs to go. But if I stay here it leaves me twenty years short of where I need to be, so I am going to Minnesota. Don't know how I'm going to break it to Mary Ellen, but we're going west. There is talk in the taverns about some newspaper man named Horace Greely who advised all young men to move west. As long as there is a west to move to, I figure you can count me in. Just don't know how I am going to tell Mary Ellen.

Chief Blackstone's Walk

I first heard the story of Blackstone's walk the summer of 1972 at Bill Rom's landing on Moose Lake. Bill Magee was in his seventies at the time and one of the best storytellers I have ever met. He was guiding people into the Quetico-Superior and could still carry a pack and canoe over the rough and rocky portages of the country he loved. People who knew him will tell you what a pleasure it was to sip Jim Beam bourbon and listen to Bill tell a story. This was one he told me:

It was a cold and rainy night in early May 1919, when there was a knock at the door. Jack Powell, the Canadian Ranger at Cache Bay who we knew so well from our Quetico travels, stood in our doorway in a checkered mackinaw and heavy duck pants. He had stopped to tell us of the death of Kawa Bay reservation and the bittersweet story of Blackstone's Walk.

My father was one of the first surgeons in Duluth, and he traveled north occasionally to doctor an injured logger and as often as possible to go fishing. We hadn't made our accustomed trip that spring because Father was much too busy taking care of the victims of the Spanish Influenza epidemic. People were dying all over the world that winter, with 500,000 succumbing to the flu in the United States alone. Father and I met and became friends with Chief Blackstone on our first trip to Kawnipi in the spring of 1912.

There was nothing exceptional I remember about the Chief which set him apart, other than the respect everyone showed him and how much stock they put in what he said. The one thing I remember when he reached down to shake my hand was looking into those deep black eyes that looked back from his hidden soul. Father believed that Blackstone was one of the last and best of the old Ojibway Chiefs. He was small in stature but tall in wisdom and spirit. When other bands gave up their timber rights to the logging companies, Blackstone refused and was branded a troublesome Indian by both government and logging officials who wanted to cut the stands of birch and pine on Kawa Bay.

After that first wonderful trip, Father and I made it our priority to head north each spring to fish for a couple of weeks on Kawnipi. Each time Father would bring with him the white man's medicine to the people of Kawa Bay. He would look down at me and say it was the least we could do after all that had been done to the Indian people since Columbus showed the rest of us the way to America.

There was nothing finer than spending a late spring evening sitting on silver-colored pine logs that had washed up on the beach long ago, looking out at Kawa Bay, as the day faded into night, and the stars tumbled out over the water.

Like most of us who looked forward to traditional things, Father and I firmly believed that we had formed a friendship with the people of Kawa Bay that was destined to last for the rest of our lives. I wish our visits could have gone on forever, but the terrible events of 1918 brought great changes to the people of Kawa Bay and the whole world, for that matter. The Spanish Influenza was the talk of the entire world as the flu unfolded its dark wings to spread its pandemic miseries across the world, reaching even out-of-the-way places like Kawnipi Lake.

Jack Powell had married a member of the Kawa Bay Band of the Ojibway, and I don't think there were any two people who felt worse over what had happened at Kawa Bay than Jack and his wife. We sat down in the kitchen and over cups of hot coffee, we listened as Jack told of the end of the Kawa Bay Reservation.

The first sign of the sickness started during the moon of the long night and came in conjunction with the first cold snap of the winter. When the coughing broke out among the people they thought at first it was just a bad cold, but it didn't take long for things to get worse. The flu quickly ran its course, descending into fevers and chills which more often than not led to pneumonia and death. With so many people sick, a council was held where it was decided that Chief Blackstone should go to Jack Powell at his government cabin on Cache Bay of Saganaga Lake.

The next morning Blackstone and his wife packed a small sled with food and rabbit skin blankets, hitched up two dogs, and set off to travel south through the unbroken snow in hopes that Jack Powell could help the people of Kawa Bay. Powell told Father that the Blackstones arrived late in the day deeply affected by the cold, and you could see that Blackstone was already sick. Powell looked at Father and remarked that it was one of the hardest things he ever did when he told the chief he had no way of getting word to the Canadian government in Ottawa. He thought their best chance would be to go where they could send a telegram asking for help.

The closest telegraphs were located in Winton, so early the next morning the Blackstones hitched up the dog team and headed Southwest. Two days later they arrived in Winton; tired, sick, and nearly exhausted. The first thing they did was to wire a telegram to the Canadian capital to let them know there was deadly sickness at Kawa Bay. Word came back from Ottawa saying, "Regret to inform Kawa Bay that people are dying all over Canada and there is currently no help available to send. Will summon resources and come at the earliest possibility."

Having nothing else to do, they started the long trek to Kawa Bay early the next morning, breaking trail through deep snow. With all the death and dying that hung in the air around them, all they could think of was going home to die with their people. From Fall Lake they crossed over to Basswood, then to Sunday, and on into Meadows, moving higher with each lake and then finally across the height of land to Canadian Agnes. They had gone nearly the whole twenty-mile length of Agnes and were just two portages short of home when Chief Blackstone collapsed and died in the snow.

His wife wrapped him in rabbit skin blankets, dragged him off the ice, and laid her husband under some balsam trees on the northeast shore of the lake. She said some quiet words over her husband and then continued her sad journey home to Kawa Bay.

After ice-out, the Canadian Rangers and Mounted Police finally made their way to Kawa Bay much too late to do any real good for most of the people who had started out the winter. By the time help arrived there were more Indians dead than living, and it was decided by the rangers to permanently close the Kawa Bay Reservation and move the remaining people to Lac La Croix. Before leaving, they took all the dead and buried them underneath the pines on the little sand mound on the northeast shore of the bay. Clearing off a large number of stones to make a place for the dead, they piled the rocks into a large cairn. As a final act of reverence they stuck a cedar cross into the cairn and said some final words over the silent dead. In a few years there was nothing left to mark the spot where they lay under the pines except a cairn of stones with a fallen cross.

Later that spring when word of Blackstone's walk spread among the bands of the Bois Forte people, they gathered at the spot where Chief Blackstone's body lay under the balsam trees and they made a proper grave house to give honor to a brave man. Entrances were made on both ends so Blackstone's spirit could travel with ease in and out of its spirit house. Around that they erected a picket fence of peeled pine, complete with a moose-hide thong gate.

Father and I once stopped there to pay our respects. We opened one of the doors and could still see the shape of the Chief's body wrapped in rabbit skins. There was a calumet, medicine bag, and bible on his chest. After a silent prayer, Father left some tobacco for the Chief's spirit.

I've been back to Kawa Bay, too. I sat by the now-cold

fire rings in the sand, and felt the spirits of the people who would never leave Kawa Bay. When you pass that way, be sure to stop in that grove of Norway pine on the little sand hill on the northeast end of the bay where the Wawiag River flows into Kawnipi, and pay your respects to the spirits of the dead by leaving them a little tobacco before you go.

The last time I visited Kawa Bay, I left tobacco for the spirits of Chief Blackstone and his people, and I also left a little extra for the spirit of my friend Bill Magee.

A Rose by Any Other Name

William Shakespeare wrote: *What's in a name? A rose by any other name would still smell as sweet.* Whenever you borrow words from someone, especially when you use them in a title, and especially when it's someone like The Bard, it only makes sense to give credit where credit is due. I did not think of the title to the story, and I didn't even think of the idea.

The other day, my friend Kevin said, "Why don't you write a story about how things got to be named around these parts." You might say that Kevin planted a seed in the ground of my head. The seed has germinated for a couple of days now, and I think it's starting to put down roots.

The first thing to admit when you start talking about how things got named is that nobody, no matter how much they know a place, can know everything there is to know about that place. It just can't be done. All this essay is meant to do is to put down, in hard copy, some of the information I have learned about how things got to be called what they are here.

To start with, the first thing people should know is how close we came to not being called Ely. The Pattison Brothers and R. B. Whiteside found iron near the south shore of Shagawa Lake in 1886. By 1888 the Chandler Mine had joined the Minnesota Mine at Soudan as the only two iron-producing mines in the state. In April of that year, people got together to incorporate as a city which meant that they had to pick a name for the place. John Pengilly was the Cornish Captain at the Chandler and he wanted the place named after his daughter

Florence. In 1888 there wasn't much here other than the Chandler Mine. It wasn't surprising to note that everyone thought Florence was a dandy name, and there wasn't a single dissenting opinion.

Luckily for those of us who have trouble spelling Ely, let alone spelling something as complicated as Florence, the name had already been taken. Fortunately, someone who spells about as poorly as I suggested we name the place Ely. The name was the last name of the first two men to buy Minnesota Iron for the eastern mills: George and Sam Ely. George was kind of dumb looking, so local history picked Sam as the historical poster boy, because he was better looking. In an interesting sidelight, Sam and George Ely even saw the town named after them. And they say we don't know how to market ourselves.

The original town site ran from Camp Street on the north to Harvey Street on the South. The Avenues ran from Central Avenue to Whiteside Park, which was then a swamp that people used as a dump. We know from an account from Mrs. Fenske, Ely's first schoolteacher, that the town was nearly wiped out by a fire heading toward the south side of the city back in 1896. The only building on the south side of the southern boundary of town was the Presbyterian Church. Shortly before the fire reached the church, the wind shifted to the east and missed the church. Rumor has it that attendance increased after this event. Members of the church felt that the pastor might have good pull where it counted.

The north boundary was called Camp Street. It was named after Asa Camp, one of the town's early mining men. If the town could boast of a hard-luck guy, I think it would be Asa Camp. The day before the first election in April of 1888, he decided to throw his hat in the ring for first mayor of the new city. He was running against Captain John Pengilly. On election eve they held a torchlight parade to rally support for Asa Camp. When the dust had settled and the votes were counted, Asa Camp fell one vote short and lost the election to Pengilly.

This first election seems to have begun a tradition of

agreeing to disagree in Ely. The tradition continues to the present. A few years later Asa Camp sold his interest in the Chandler Mine for $25,000 to the banker Joseph Sellwood. Asa Camp moved to Seattle, Washington. Asa Camp died a pauper, and Joseph Sellwood ended up a millionaire.

In an interesting side note, Mrs. Asa Camp – women in those days didn't have first names in the newspapers – was the first woman to run for office in the city. Women could not vote or run for office in any federal, state, or local election, but the school district did not exclude women running for office in its bylaws. In the fall of 1899 Mrs. Camp and forty women marched into the room where elections were held, and demanded to be put on the ballot. The event was so shocking that three members of the board resigned on the spot.

When the votes were counted, Mrs. Camp didn't win a seat on the school board, but she carried the women's vote. The school board changed its bylaws. It would be over twenty years before women would vote again in an Ely election. What Mr. Camp felt about the incident remains a mystery.

Ely's main street, referred to as the main drag when I was growing up, is Sheridan Street. At one time I thought it might be named after Phil Sheridan, the Civil War cavalry general. When I looked into it further, I found out the street was named after James Sheridan. James Sheridan was a partner of Asa Camp and they were both partners in the early development of the Chandler Mine. Other than having the main street named after him, James Sheridan had the honor of being the oldest of the town's settlers born in 1829. Sheridan's latest honor was having the dining room at Vertin's Café named for him.

There were only two streets that weren't named after a person. One of those was Chapman Street. It took me a long time before I was able to figure out where the name came from, but I could find no reference to a Mr. Chapman in the town's old newspapers. One of the things about questions is that if you keep asking enough, someone will be able to give you an answer, probably later than sooner. Finally an old friend of

English extraction told me the name *Chapman* was English slang for businessmen. The businessmen had to go somewhere, so they put them as far south of the mine as practical. It doesn't take much imagination to see how small the town was in the beginning. The business street was just over two blocks long.

Contrary to the opinion of some, who stick to the idea that Harvey Street was named after the invisible rabbit in the Jimmy Stewart movie, the street takes its name from H. G. Harvey. Harvey was the mining man who ran the diamond drill for the Pattison Brothers back in 1885-86. I don't think they could have mined iron on the Vermilion Range if it wasn't for the diamond drill, which acted as the miners' eyes and allowed them to read the difficult iron formation. The iron in Ely and Soudan was "stood on end" millions of years ago. The only way to find how it ran was by reading the hollow core samples that enabled the miners to map out the formation. H. G. Harvey was an important man in determining the success of the venture, and that's what happens; they name a street after you.

Looking for room to grow, the town started to spread to the south. The next street to develop was Conan and it was named after Ely resident Dr. Conan, who did not practice medicine in Ely. He was both a doctor and an engineer. Engineering was his occupation during his residence in Ely. The hospital was named after its owner, Charles Shipman. I guess the people of the town didn't want Conan to feel slighted, so they named a street after him. Sorry folks, I just couldn't stretch things as far as naming it after Conan the Barbarian.

The only thing I could come up with for how White Street got named is that it took its name from James White, one of the prominent members of the business community. A picture, in both Lee Brownell's and Shammy Somrock's history books, shows the town's shooting club. You didn't get to be a member of the sportsman's club unless you were somebody, and one of the names on the picture is James White.

I have a lot more information about how the next two streets were named. The next street south of White Street was named in honor of Abbija James. James came to Ely before the rail road was finished, and had to walk the last five miles into town. When he got to town he was suffering from the early symptoms of a fever and lay down on a bench in the lobby of the Exchange Hotel. Dr. Shipman passed the unconscious man on his way to breakfast. When the doctor noticed James still lying on the bench when he went to dinner, Dr. Shipman went over and found Abbija James burning up with fever. Dr. Shipman nursed James back to health only to find out that he was a druggist by trade, which was something the doctors in town needed badly. Abbija James went on to found Ely's longest running business, the James Drug store, which stayed open until the late 1990s.

One street further south and you come to Pattison Street. Martin and Richard Pattison led the first exploration of the site, which would someday come to be known as Ely, in the spring of 1886. They came by railroad from Duluth to Tower that spring, and from there, they hired a small number of French Canadians to haul equipment twenty miles east of Soudan to the south shore of Shagawa Lake. They traveled by water and portage from Lake Vermilion through Mud Creek, into Burntside Lake where they followed the river into Shagawa. Finding the iron was no small task and it took a second season before they were able to pinpoint the non-magnetic high grade iron with the help of H. G. Harvey's diamond drill.

To give you some idea of how much money was made by the Pattison Brothers from their Ely venture, the fees paid out to them from the late 1880s until the early 1920s were around $185,000 a month. Of that, over $100,000 was clear profit. With that kind of money, you get a street named after you. The southern expansion stopped one block south of Pattison Street, and being the practical people we are, the founding fathers reached deeply into their imaginations and said, "Why don't we call it Boundary Street." They did.

The town also expanded to the east after the start of the twentieth century and if you notice, both Camp Street and Sheridan Street are crooked. Instead of running straight they both take a turn to the North. If I made a guess why, it would be that outcroppings of greenstone blocked the way. Like most of the rock around these parts, greenstone is a hard rock to drill and blast. I think they bent the road to save time and money. That's in part because the land east of Whiteside Park was purchased by a private investor who decided to do the surveying by himself. This is a prime example of the phrase that you get what you pay for. It is interesting to note that as we write this today, it will be the first time in its history that Camp Street, which is actually a county road, will have curbs and gutters.

To be fair to the town's north-enders, there are a couple of streets north of Camp Street that were added to the town after it was first incorporated. Chandler Road was added after it was discovered that Captain Pengilly's house was outside the city limits. He had to resign his position as mayor of the city. Not to be denied, the good Captain led the charge for annexation. He was able to make a comeback and once again served as mayor of the city.

There is one avenue of note that I would like to mention, which gives honor to Matt Stukel. It is called Stukel Way and it runs from Harvey to Pattison Streets. There is an old saying which says that big things come in small packages, and I think it describes Stukel Way perfectly. It isn't so much how long it is, but it's more a case of where it runs. Stukel Way starts at the corner of the Little League Field and ends where Veterans' Field meets Pattison Street. There have been many people who have helped keep baseball alive and vital here at the end of the road, but nobody did more than Matt Stukel. Matt Stukel is the only person I knew who had a street named in his honor, and I think I know why. I couldn't hit a beach ball with a tennis racket, but you didn't have to be a ball player to get a kind word from Matt Stukel. Matt Stukel was not only nice to the boys who played ball, he was nice to everyone. That's how you get a street named after you.

We have two parks in town. The one everyone knows about is Whiteside Park, because it sits right on the main street of town, and is the place that plays host to most of the summer's social functions. The park was named after the man who donated it to the city, R. B. Whiteside. R. B. Whiteside put up the funding for the two expeditions that the Pattison Brothers led in the mid-1880s to locate iron. One of the things that Whiteside doesn't get credit for is the land where the baseball, practice, and girls softball fields are located. This land was also given to the city by R. B. Whiteside.

The second park, the one that mostly local people know about and use, is Semer's Park which has served for many years as the town's swimming beach. The park takes its name from James Semer, a Michigan speculator who bought the land back in the 1890s. When Semer found that there was no iron on the property, he donated the land to the City of Ely. It might not have been much of a gift back then, but when I look around at the price of lake shore, I wonder just what the value of Big and Little Islands, and all that lakeshore, might be in today's terms.

One of the best additions to our city has been the Trezona Trail, which runs just over four miles around Miners Lake. Miners Lake lies on the north edge of the city. The trail is part of a greater system that runs all the way from Ely to Grand Rapids. The system was paid for by the Iron Range Resources and Rehabilitation Board (now know as Iron Range Resources). They should know that, at least in Ely, their work has been greatly appreciated, and extremely successful.

Unlike most of the trail system, the Trezona Trail is for non-motorized use only. If you are in town and are thinking of taking a walk, cycle, cross-country ski, or a good jog, why not think about the Trezona Trail? It starts on the west end of town, a block and a half north of two fine restaurants and an outfitting shop where you can rent a bike or pair of cross country skis. Should you run out of gas, you can take a room at the Grand Ely Lodge, which is just a stone's throw off the trail. If you're interested in wolves, you can take the Stenlund Spur to the International Wolf Center. The Stenlund Spur heads south from the Trezona, just over a quarter mile where it crosses Highway 169 and leads a short distance further to the center. At the Wolf Center, you can learn about and see live wolves.

The Trezona Trail is named for Ely's most dominant mine captain, Charlie Trezona, who ran the operations for the Oliver Iron Mining Company for thirty years. The Stenlund Spur was named for Milt Stenlund who was born in Ely, wrote several books about the town, and ran the first real scientific study of timber wolves in the state of Minnesota.

If you count the dispensary above the old James Drug Store on the corner of Chapman Street and First Avenue, Ely has had three hospitals. The first hospital was named after its owner, Dr. Shipman, and stood on the southeast corner of Chapman and Second Avenue right across the street from city hall. The Shipman Hospital was a three-story structure of Victorian design. It is interesting to note that the building was designed by Dr. Shipman's father, who had designed the capital dome for the state of Wisconsin in Madison. The Shipman Hospital was torn down in the 1960s to make room for the clinic, which was built just to the east of the hospital at the same time the Shipman was coming down.

I still remember standing on the East Side of the Shipman Hospital, looking up at one of my new cousins as the nurse held the baby up to the window on the third story of the hospital. At that distance they all looked like my grandpa – toothless and bald. That's where the nursery was, on the third floor of the hospital, and that's as close as any kid got to a baby. They kept babies and new mothers in the Shipman Hospital for about a week, and no kids were allowed, because they didn't want to expose the baby to any unwanted germs.

Ely's second hospital was constructed on the corner of Second Avenue and Camp Street in 1903 and opened for business in 1904. It was originally called the Tanner Hospital and was named after its owner and builder, Anterro Tanner. Anterro Tanner was an outspoken socialist who published several newspapers that were aimed at bettering the state of workers. He started one in Ely in 1906 which lasted just three issues. There wasn't enough room for a socialist newspaper in a mining town, and Anterro Tanner sold his hospital to a Dr. Carpenter the same year. I don't know how long it ran as the Carpenter Hospital.

When I was growing up, the old hospital was called the Lake View Apartments, but it has been closed now for many years. The old Tanner Hospital building is still standing on the corner of Second and Camp and the kids in town call it the castle. It is still a fine building, and it is still in good shape. Anterro Tanner was a good man who built a beautiful building, and he built it well. I hope someone comes to town and buys the Tanner Hospital. The town wouldn't be the same without it.

Our third hospital opened in the late 1950s and is still offering quality medical services for people around the entire area. The idea of a modern hospital was advocated first by Dr. Harry Sutherland. Sutherland practiced medicine in Ely for many years, and is credited with delivering over a thousand babies during the time he served Ely. The man who really pushed for the new hospital was Dr. J. P. Grahek. Doc Grahek owned the Shipman Hospital and practiced medicine there. Nobody knew better how outdated the old hospital was, and how badly we needed a new facility.

After many debates and some stiff opposition, mostly from people who backed Dr. Omar Snyker and the Winton Hospital, it was finally agreed that the city would build a state-of-the-art medical facility to better serve the needs of the people. The money that put the project over the top was a one hundred thousand dollar gift from Abe Bloomenson, an old ex-Ely businessman who still cared about the place. In honor of the gift, they named the hospital the Ely Bloomenson. Since then the Bloomenson Hospital has grown to include two nursing homes, and a nearby apartment complex. One has to wonder where all of our people would have gone, had not Doc Grahek pushed for all these things that have made Ely a better place to live.

Talking about names is something that could go on for a long time, and there are lots of other names we could talk about, but that can wait for another time. If you know anything about the names that have been talked about here, why not drop me a line at the *Timberjay* and let me know what you know about how things got named. All I really know is that we need more people like Dane Sorenson, who came to town, invested in several buildings, and named one after our old elementary school principal Alvin Sorenson. Now that's the kind of community spirit we need.

The Hanged Man's Tree

The proper wording for it would be the Hanged Man's Tree, I think, but to all the kids in town, the cement stump, with a rope holding some sort of scroll with a name and date on it, was referred to as the Hang Man's Tree. The name on the stone read Samuel V. Brown. He was born in Cornwall in the 1870s and had come to seek his fortune in the New World. Sam Brown died in the spring of 1895 from what every person in town thought was suicide. The reason they believed it was suicide was because of the rope that held up the scroll with all the pertinent information on it. There wasn't a person in town who didn't believe that Sam Brown committed suicide.

There was another tree stump grave marker in the local cemetery. It didn't have a rope on it, but if Sam Brown's marker meant that a person had hung themselves, then surely it must mean that Shaefer, the only name on the hollowed-out metal stump, must have committed suicide as well. But this is where you cross into dangerous thinking. It's the point where you start drawing conclusions, because somebody told you something and you think it's true. But I'm finding out what you think is true, and what is true, can be very different.

One of the legends that grew up around the metal stump, with the name Shaefer on it, was that the family was so distraught by the suicide of one of their loved ones that they buried all that person's most precious possessions with them in the hollowed-out metal stump. Even so, when we went to look at the metal stump, shortly before sunset, we were waiting for the vampire to come out of the old vault. We had gone to a Hammer vampire film earlier that summer, and Christopher Lee was some kind of Dracula. He stuck in your mind. My friends and I thought that he had moved to Ely and was living in the old brick vault, which used to stand at the bottom of the hill at the west end of the cemetery. Uncle Poochey used to tell people the reason they had to tear down the old vault was that it didn't have a fire escape. But we all knew it was because there was a vampire in the vault who might be worse than Christopher Lee.

One night when we were waiting for the sun to set, and to have Dracula come out of the old vault, we went over to the other Hanged Man's Grave. Even though there were a lot of us there that night, we were nervous about the old vault. If there was a place made for a vampire it was the old vault in our cemetery. It was made well of deep brownish-red bricks. They were the good kind. Nobody wanted to short change the dead by purchasing bricks of poor quality, so the building had just the right touch of class to it. Ivy grew from the north and east walls, and the windows were boarded up. If that wasn't enough, there were even bars on the windows. We always wondered what the bars were for.

When we were waiting for the sun to set, and the vampire to come out of the old vault, we went over to the metal stump. One of my friends, I honestly don't remember which one, brought a wrench to see if we could get the last bolt off of the plaque with the name Shaefer on it. Three of the original four bolts had already been removed. But that bolt was crossthreaded and stripped, and no matter how hard we tried to remove that last bolt and to get our hands on Shaefer's most prized possession, that final bolt is still in place. It is a comfort to know that you were not the first to bite into the legend of treasure inside a hollow metal stump, but that wasn't the first time we bit into something like that. We never got the bolt off, and we never made it to the sunset to see the vampire come out of the old vault. Someone got scared just before sunset and took off on their bike, heading back to the safety of town, and before long they were joined by everyone else, because nobody wanted to end up being a snack for Drac.

My mother and her younger sister told us that the gypsies used to come to the west end of town when she was a girl; to dance and sing and to tell fortunes. There was nowhere else for them to come to. There was nowhere else for anyone to come to, unless you were a Canadian, an Indian, or someone who was extremely lost. Mother and Auntie Evie told us that the gypsies made so much money that they buried some in wooden chests. The gypsies would come back for the money when no one was looking for them. Mother and my aunt told us that sometimes if you went up into the pine woods on the west end of town, you could see where the gypsies buried their treasure.

It was a great story that they enjoyed telling year after year. I don't think either of them thought we would take them seriously, but kids are more gullible than we care to give them credit for, and my friends and I were at the top of the list.

What we didn't know was that the woods on the west end of town, where the old pines grew in the big sand bank, were once the town's old cemetery. Many of the original tenants were moved to the new cemetery on the east end of town, but some of the older tenants were too far gone to move, and were left where they were. The pines were planted over them in 1943 as a memorial to the service people who were fighting in World War Two. That's the reason why they can't dig any more gravel from the banks. Those trees are part of a memorial forest. Years ago, some women from the women's auxiliary came before the town council and told the council they would sue the city if one more tree fell, because they continued to dig from the bank. The city hasn't dug a thing since.

My aunt and uncle's house was less than three blocks from those woods, and on a day when we were playing at being Robin Hood out in Sherwood Forest, we came upon several suspicious indentations in the ground. They seemed to fit the description Mother and Auntie had told us of buried gypsy treasure. In our minds' eyes we could almost see the rotted old wooden chest that the gypsies had buried there earlier. All of us were sure that in a short time, we would be richer than anyone of us had ever imagined. It was like something out of Tom Sawyer and Huck Finn.

We rushed down the hill to Uncle Tony's Garage. Uncle Tony was a quiet man, with a ton of useful tools. We took two shovels and a pick, loaded them into his wheelbarrow, and wheeled them back up the hill to claim our treasure.

We dug for what seemed to be forever, all the time expecting to come in contact with a box filled with loot. Then we found a woman's shoe that laced up the side, and looked as if it came from the turn of the century. Instead of gypsy treasure, we had been digging in one of the old graves that remained when they moved the old cemetery. We dropped the pick and shovels, left the wheelbarrow where it was, and we headed down the hill as fast as we left the new cemetery before sunset when the vampire was going to come out.

Uncle Tony noticed that the tools we had hauled up the hill a short time earlier had not made the return trip, and he asked us what had happened to his tools. After a short interrogation we told him that we thought we were digging for gypsy treasure but that instead of that, we had been digging in an old grave, and we had dug up an old shoe.

Uncle Tony made us go back into the woods and show him were we had been digging. He made us put the old shoe back into the grave, and then we filled it back in. Before we left Uncle Tony had us say some words over the grave, and we all felt bad about disturbing her rest. It may have been the only time in history that words of prayer and apology were said over a shoe. It was the last time we ever dug for treasure of any kind.

The way I found out about the hanged man's trees at the new cemetery came years later when I was working as a mine guide at the Soudan Underground Mine State Park. They referred to the Soudan Mine as a Cadillac, because it was such a good place to work. The rock was so solid they didn't need to timber any of the tunnels the men dug in order to get to the iron, and it was also a very dry mine. Good rock and little water made it a fine place to work. The mining done twenty miles away in Ely was altogether different. The rock was busted into pieces, and they were pumping over two million gallons of water a day to keep the mine from filling with water. I knew that there were many accidents, and one day in order to satisfy my curiosity I went to the city hall and started to go through the death records to see how many men had actually died in the Ely Mines. In all the years of operation, only thirteen men died at the Soudan Mine. This was quite a contrast with over one hundred and forty who were killed in the mines that operated in Ely.

The city kept records of everyone who died in Ely from the 1890s until the early 1950s, which is how I finally discovered the truth about Samuel V. Brown. I was going through the ledger for 1895 and when I got to May of that year, imagine my surprise when I got to the entry for Sam Brown, and I read "died of natural causes." I couldn't believe my eyes. At first I thought they might have entered it that way to protect his family's feelings, but just to make sure I went back to the old newspapers to see if they wouldn't shed some more light on the mystery.

The first information I found was that in January of that year he had brought his sweetheart over from England, and the whole town turned out for the celebration. It was hard to think that he only had a few months to live, but when I got to May, there on the front page was the sad news that Sam Brown had died at home of natural causes. Here this poor fellow had lain in the cemetery for over a hundred years underneath the hanged man's tree, with everyone in town believing he had committed suicide. Could that mean that the other hanged man was also innocent of taking his own life?

I went back into the death records and found that the person lying under the second metal stump was a young man of fifteen, Christian Schaefer, who died at home the day before Christmas, from natural causes. I thought how ironic it was that the two men who everyone thought killed themselves didn't. People saw the rope on Sam Brown's headstone, and drew the conclusion that Sam Brown must have hung himself. When I looked into what the headstones of a tree stump really meant, our local undertaker told me that a tree stump marked the spot of a young person who had been cut off in the prime of life, and did not mark a suicide. I don't suppose it makes much difference what people think about you after you're dead, but I think I would rest a little easier with people finally learning the truth about how I died. If there is a lesson to learn from all this I believe it would be that you can't always believe what people tell you, and sometimes stories grow up about someone that are far from the truth. It is easy to fancy the spirits of those two men smiling about finally being cleared of the cloud of suicide that clung to them for so many years.

Anterro F. Tanner

The man who designed and built the old hospital couldn't have picked a better time for members of the town's historic preservation committee to see his work. The time was right at the end of a cloudy December day. We were gathered there, and just as the sun was about to go down, it broke through the layer of stratus clouds that had dominated the day. The moment the sun came in through the large bank of windows, the whole countenance of the place changed.

None of us had ever seen the inside of the building open as if it was intended to be when it was a hospital. When my sister and her family had lived there, the building was known as The Lake View Apartments. They were small one and two bedroom units. These units fragmented the original intentions of the architect and builder who envisioned a place of light and beauty.

Watching the sun set through the windows, and seeing the place open and well lit the way Anterro Tanner designed it, made me sad to think that such a beautiful old building would probably come down in a few years if something wasn't done to save it.

Like most small towns, the people who serve on committees such as historical preservation care about their community, and the special places that make it what it is. Everyone knows places like the Tanner Hospital should be saved, but no one has the money to save it. Places like my hometown will be lucky to save their city hall, community center, and library.

There don't seem to be any other resources left for the other old places that are standing on time and waiting for the wrecking ball. Standing there in that still-solid building, and watching the sun set over Shagawa Lake, made me wonder just who it was that took the time to build such a beautiful place.

Anterro Ferdinand Tanner was born in Finland on May 6, 1868. During his life he had served as a hired hand, clerk, apprentice shoemaker, teacher, physician, lecturer, writer, publisher, newspaper editor and owner, architect, and social activist – a truly remarkable man. He was a man who looked to the future, social change, and a chance for new ideas. It was this insatiable drive for new ideas that forced him to come to America.

There were several forces at work in the 1880s, which conspired to drive many free-thinkers such as Anterro Tanner from Finland. The first thing was Russia's February 1889 Manifesto which negated Finland's status as a self-governing grand-duchy. Russia claimed power to make laws governing the Finish people, and the right to draft Finns into the Russian army. They would not allow any reference to Finland on postage stamps, and many Finns, such as the Helsinki University-educated Tanner, were concerned for the future of Finnish culture.

The second factor influencing Tanner's decision to come to America came from the Finnish Church. Unlike America, which recognizes no church over any other, and maintains a separation of church and state, Finland only recognized the Finnish state church, which everyone had been forced to join. In 1889 legislation was passed that allowed people to leave the state church, but it only allowed them to join another Protestant denomination. These churches provided much control over the daily lives of the Finn people. One could not be married without permission from the church, and in order to get a passport you had to obtain a letter of character from the parish church. Some people could live under such stringent conditions, but Anterro Tanner was not numbered among them.

There was a class system in place designed to keep

people in their proper places, which placed an unfair burden on the working class. If you were born a working man, you were expected to die a working man, and follow in the footsteps of your father. There seemed little hope for advancement for the lower classes. The church told people to forget material goods, and to realize that suffering is part of life and cannot be avoided. But there were a few people who started to speak up against such things, and the socialist movement – *a social system where the producers possess both political power and the means of producing and distributing goods* – was born.

When Anterro Tanner became a popular speaker for the new movement, he gained the attention of both the church, and the Russian rulers who wanted to put an end to the bothersome and threatening socialist movement. When word of his possible arrest reached Tanner in 1899, he decided to sail for America and the freedom America was supposed to represent.

He settled in Rockport Massachusetts and bumped into an old schoolmate who had become a pastor. The pastor invited Tanner to deliver a series of lectures to the Finnish community. Tanner spoke on many topics regarding the natural sciences, and even had the audacity to introduce the idea of Darwin's theory of evolution. The pastor accused Tanner of being a socialist, but instead of backing down from the conflict, Tanner asked if he might not be able to speak to the people in order to explain just what socialism was. The pastor demanded that Tanner publicly reaffirm his faith. Anterro Tanner flatly refused. He responded by saying, "In twentieth-century America, the land of freedom, a Finnish clergyman who denies a university-trained man to speak thus withholds from his congregation the right of higher learning." The people agreed with Tanner, and thus came an unexpected turn in his life. He became an active and effective writer and speaker for the socialist cause in America.

In 1900 Tanner formed a partnership, with his friend Martin Hendrickson, to publish a newspaper *The American Tyomies; The American Worker,* which went to print in January of that year. The mission of the paper was to get across to enough people that there were many things wrong with the world, and there were changes that needed to be made. There was never enough money to sustain the paper, so Tanner decided to take a tour of the Midwest in order to obtain subscriptions to the *Tyomie*. He was called the devil's advocate, the deceiver of his country, an anarchist, an atheist, and was often denied places to speak, eat, and sleep. But none of that ever stopped Anterro Tanner: *"The reason nevertheless, for the opposition I faced, was not religion. I avoided discussion of church and clergy. The cause to the fury was opposition to new ideas."* What stopped Anterro Tanner was lack of money.

Along with seeking subscribers, Tanner was also looking for a new home for the *American Worker*. With its sizeable Finn population, Tanner, Hendrickson, and the other stockholders of the paper decided that Minneapolis would be the best place. Tanner moved his family to Minnesota by train. No sooner had he arrived than word came from Massachusetts that the shareholders had decided they could no longer afford to print the paper.

Although he was tired out from the whole experience, Tanner continued to write articles for other papers, and was active in many small discussion groups. While in Minneapolis, he went back to school and passed his doctor's examination from The University of Minnesota.

Dr. Tanner brought his family to Ely in the fall of 1902. In 1903 he and his wife Venni bought two lots on Camp Street when they decided to make Ely their home. By the end of that year, people in town watched as one of the truly unique buildings in town began to take shape. A castle-like tower dominated the north end of the brick structure, and the word "Hospital" was printed boldly across the front of the building. *The Ely Miner* described the Tanner Hospital as an up-to-date medical facility with a lab and dispensary, and special attention given to surgery.

The interior had been designed for convenience, light, and ventilation. Dr. Tanner firmly believed that if a sick or injured person was put in a place of light and beauty they would feel better and heal faster. The building's circular tower was where patients went after surgery, because it was private, and you could see all of Shagawa Lake from the tower. The hospital was steam heated, electric powered, and could comfortably handle up to twenty patients.

The Tanners were active members of the community and many people remembered the nights where Venni Tanner would sing in her simple and pure soprano voice. They remembered Anterro Tanner as a short man, inclined toward being chunky with a pock-marked face. Tanner was quite the showman, wearing his black velvet knee pants with bows at the knees. The other dominant feature of his apparel was a bright purple vest.

One night when he was at the Finnish Opera House lecturing on the wonders of science, Tanner brought fourth a bottle of clear odorless liquid that he invited members of the audience to examine. They looked at it, smelled it, and tasted it before they came to the conclusion that what Dr. Tanner had in the glass jar was water. Then Tanner passed his hand over the jar and lit a match. The water burned brightly in the center of the jar, which caused an involuntary gasp from the entire audience. Probably the only people who were aware that the liquid must have been potassium were the town druggist and some of the chemists who worked at the mine.

Patients who went into surgery remembered a pock-marked face and a man with a kindly voice and manners, who inspired confidence in his patients. In a humorous moment, people remembered the day they went to the hospital to watch Anterro Tanner knock out bricks around the main door of the hospital.

The Tanners had a summer home on Shagawa Lake and Doc Tanner wanted to have a boat so that he could go fishing. Being the handyman he was, rather than hiring someone else to build the boat, he decided to do it himself in the hospital's basement. People said it was a fine boat, and everything went well until they tried to carry the boat out of the hospital. In a case of mis-measuring, Tanner had made the boat slightly bigger than the door. As in most small towns, word of the doctor's predicament spread quickly, and everyone who had a moment made it a point to stop by the Tanner Hospital to watch Doc Tanner knock bricks out from around his door.

Tanner could not stick just to being a doctor and lecturer at the Opera House. In 1905, seeing a need for a Finnish newspaper, he invited his old friend Martin Hendrickson back to town in order to get things started. Tanner invited one hundred-fifty members of the business community and clergy to the Opera House to discuss the need for a good paper. After five days of discussion, Hendrickson declined the offer and decided to continue on his speaking tour of America. But Tanner did go on to produce a paper and that year he printed the first edition of *Aatietta; Thoughts.* The paper lasted only three months. Some Thoughts in Ely, Minnesota could be thought, and other Thoughts were taboo.

In the first decade of the 1900s it was hard to support a socialistic paper anywhere in America. In Ely it was impossible. The town was run by mining men like Captain Charlie Trezona, who was in charge of the mining interests of The Oliver Iron Mining Company, United States Steel. Captain Charlie had nearly been lynched by radicals less than three years before. Good or bad, Captain Charlie controlled the town. There is little doubt that Captain Charlie let the hundreds of men who worked for him in the mines know that it would not be well received by Captain Charlie if any friend of his showed support for a socialist. If you were one of the men who worked in the mines, you were afraid that if you supported *Aatteita,* or were seen at the Tanner Hospital, you might not have a job in the mines.

From a business standpoint, while you might support Anterro Tanner's high moral principles, one could not afford to be linked with anything such as socialism. Every businessman knew that taking out an advertisement in Tanner's paper would be risking their business for a principle, and not many were willing to take that risk. In 1906 Anterro Tanner and his family left town, and there was nothing left to remember them by except the eccentric building that stands on the corner of Second Avenue and Camp Street.

The Tanners went back to Finland for a time, and Venni Tanner disappeared from the story. When war clouds began to gather, and Czarist Russia mustered its Finnish vassals, Anterro Tanner decided to come back to America. In 1920 he was living in Chisholm, Minnesota, and was in the process of building a glass hospital. Tanner believed it would be a thing of beauty, which would also pay for itself by using solar power. With coal as cheap as it was, many people thought he was crazy.

On November 27, 1920, Anterro Tanner died of pneumonia in Chisholm, and with him died any dream of a glass hospital. Together he and his nurse Ulla Maria had adopted a baby girl, and when Tanner died, she and the baby went back east. Several years after Tanner's death they returned to Chisholm and are buried in a common plot in the Chisholm cemetery.

All this came to me in a moment. From the time the sun freed itself from the clouds, until the last of it dipped beneath the horizon, I could feel the presence of Anterro Tanner. When the twilight faded and the stars started to tumble out, I could feel him standing there at the close of day. The story of the hospital and the man who thought and built it were played out before me. I thought it a shame to lose such a rich story.

The moment the sun left the room, all the magic of Anterro Tanner was gone. Now was the time of day when they would fire up the boiler, and turn on the electric lights, because the sun had gone to bed. There were no lights or boiler to light this December night, but when we left the room I could feel the spirit of a portly ghost, with a pock-marked face and a kindly spirit. How sad it would be to forget a man who thought too much, dreamed too much, cared too much, and fought too hard. It would be nice to save his hospital, I thought. Then we all went home.

Christmas Trees

Perhaps it was a holdover from the Depression, or maybe it was the power of tradition, but picking out a good Christmas tree was one of the things Dad always took care of for our family. One tough winter when an early November blizzard dumped two feet of snow out in the woods, I suggested that we go down to the lumberyard and buy our Christmas tree. Dad gave me a shocked look and told me that he didn't believe in buying a Christmas tree, just like he didn't approve of buying fish. As long as they were out there for the getting, then, by God, that is what we were going to do.

We ended up putting on the snowshoes that year, and breaking trail through the deep snow to get to the stand of balsam that he had scouted out earlier that season. I can still hear him muttering to himself about not getting out early enough, and how old man winter had caught him with his pants down. "Mikey," he said, "let this be a lesson to you. In the future we will always get the jump on winter, and never let this happen again." The next spring we started looking for a Christmas tree as soon as the woods opened up.

Dad loved to drive the old roads. He and Mother would pack a picnic lunch and head out to some remote trail. They would stop at a favorite spot for an extended lunch, then continue down some old gravel road heading to anywhere. It really didn't matter to them where they were going, as long as they were out in the woods. Those trips started to turn into travel adventures as Mother and Dad blazed new trails. Mother told me about driving over old wooden bridges that were so worn and narrow that she had to get out and guide Dad to position the tires so that they wouldn't break through. I asked her once what she would do if they broke down out there. She smiled and said that God watched out for people such as her and Dad, and if they broke down, someone was bound to find them sometime. I wasn't much reassured, but limited my comments to requesting that they always leave a note telling us the basic direction they were heading.

While they were driving, Dad kept an eye out for anything interesting, such as a potential Christmas tree. He would enter his observations in a little book. By the end of summer, there were usually several candidates on Dad's Christmas tree list. After that, it was a matter of picking the style to fit the mood of that particular season.

Many people considered only a spruce or balsam for their Christmas tree, but Dad was not restricted by such conventions. One season, in a moment of inspiration, Dad said maybe it would be nice to have a Norway pine for a change of pace. Mother thought it would be refreshing to have something other than a traditional spruce or balsam. I can still remember that small red pine standing resplendent in our living room, giving our family a new perspective on what constituted a good Christmas tree. From that time on, about the only thing mother would ask of Dad was that whatever type of tree he brought home for her to decorate, it would still be green. One autumn day, sitting at the kitchen table, Dad asked me how I thought a tamarack tree would look in the tree stand. Mother turned from the stove and told him in no uncertain terms that something without needles was not an option.

"Look for a good three-quarter tree," Dad would say. "You're not going to get much more than that because everything in the world has a bad side, and Christmas trees are no exception." Sometimes Dad would see a "fifty-fifty" tree. This meant that half the tree was fine while the other side looked pretty sparse. "If we face the bad side to the wall this little spruce will make a grand site once Mother puts on the decorations," Dad would say. One year, after we had finished decorating the tree, Mother echoed Dad's philosophy, saying that people were a lot like Christmas trees because we all have a good and bad side and that it was important to be sure it was your best side that faced the world.

Once Dad brought a tree home, it was up to Mother to decorate it. But over the years Dad had a few objections. One year while Dad was out, Mother flocked the tree with fake snow. When Dad came home he let Mother know that if she planned to smother one of his trees in Sears and Roebuck snow again, she should look for someone else to bring the tree home. Then there was the year she sheeted the tree with icicles. Dad said we might as well have a tamarack or birch next year. Mom never again flocked or sheeted one of Dad's beautiful trees. The only other point of contention arose when twinkle lights first came out. Dad came home from work and there was the Christmas tree blinking away in the living room. He walked over and turned off the blinker setting then stated that when they really twinkle he'd be glad to watch them twinkle, but blinking made him nervous. Bubbling lights were tolerable, but mostly our trees were either on or off.

I don't know how many Christmas trees Dad picked out over the years. It was something he started with his grandfather and ended with his grandchildren eight decades later. I went along with Dad and my kids a couple of times. Dad had become so sophisticated about it that he wouldn't let on that he knew of a beautiful tree down a certain old road. He'd let the kids lead the way while he followed them with the small camp saw he always kept sharp. Then the kids would round the corner and there, in a small open patch of forest, would be a Christmas tree that was too good to pass up. The kids would scream with delight that they had found the Christmas tree, and they would come running to grandpa to show him where it was. When they arrived at "their" tree he would look down on them, smile, and tell them that they were just about the best tree finders ever.

It's been six years since Dad took the kids to pick out a

Christmas tree. I'm not as good at it as he was, but sometime between Halloween and Thanksgiving, I'll go out and choose a nice looking tree that is perfect in its imperfection. I'll come back home, put it up, face its bad side to the wall and its good side to the world, and think about my family. Then I'll adorn it with many of the same old decorations that Mother collected over the years. I'll wait for my daughter to come home and share the memories, as in so many other homes in Ely and the world, our tree lights linking us with our past, present, and future.

Miss Dahl

Several people have told me that under normal circumstances, the mind does not allow us to dwell on negative thoughts. I remember asking my dad, a few weeks before he died, how he was doing. Dad looked up from his workbench and told me he was slowing down, but couldn't remember having a bad day. I lived with him long enough to know that like all of us, Dad had his ups and downs. He had some bad days. But I believe Dad was being honest with me.

Most of the time when we look back on our lives, we remember the good times. It's just the way the mind is set up. If we were keyed toward the negative, none of us would want to make seventy. But there are times when even the most pleasant of thoughts can trigger something in us which allows those not-so-pleasant memories to come flooding back. Most of the time we try to keep the memory lid clamped down tight, but then there are those moments, when the lid pops open and out they come.

I was telling stories down in Austin, Minnesota a few years back. One of the tellers on the program was a cowboy from Oklahoma named Michael Johnson. He was a sparse man with a weathered face. The dress was mostly denim. The hat was a black Stetson. Michael spoke in one of those clipped Texas dialects that sounded a little like Sam Elliot. He was talking about a lady by the name of Miss Ida who made a great impression on him and helped shape the course of his life.

Miss Ida was Michael Johnson's first grade teacher.

Miss Ida was one of those southern women who talked sweet. Her students were called names like Sugar and Sweetness. They are nicknames that can only be used by southern women. Their northern counterparts would have a difficult time calling one of their men Sugar Cakes. It is a syrupy kind of talk that starts to feel sticky to me after a short time. Sweet talk wears thin on northern men, because our women don't talk to us like that. About the closest I remember a northern woman talking sugar was when my ex-wife's grandmother would call Grandpa Honey Bunch. Maybe I'm just jealous. When I heard Michael Johnson talking about Miss Ida, I wished I could have been that young cowboy who climbed into her lap at the end of a hard day and had someone sounding like something out of *Gone With The Wind* talk sweet and kind to me.

By the time I met Michael Johnson, Miss Ida had already been in heaven for a long time, but she still talked sweet talk to Michael and he still listened. Miss Ida was one of those people you meet who you hear talking in the back of your mind forever. I think Miss Ida provided a lot of the foundation that was at the very bottom of what Michael was all about. Whenever life provided challenges to him, it was Miss Ida and her wonderful teaching that he would come back to. There was not a doubt in his mind that somewhere up on some beautiful cloud, Miss Ida was watching him. Much of the moral fiber and rightness associated with the integrity of cowboys comes from people like Miss Ida. While I sat there, it made me think about *My* first grade teacher, Miss Dahl.

The first thing crossing my mind was that I never in my life pictured Miss Dahl sitting on a cloud, looking down on me from heaven. It would have been a good-sized cloud. The Miss Dahl who existed in my mind was one of the largest women I could remember. If there was a cloud for Miss Dahl, it would have to be one of those big clouds that anvil out on the top of the sky. Anyone who knew her would tell you that it would take a heck of a big cloud to support Stella Dahl, and you could just bet it would be spitting lightning and rumbling thunder.

Miss Dahl walked down the aisles of my first grade

class, carrying a quarter-inch thick yardstick, made of real wood, and looking for all the world like one of those balloons from the New York City Thanksgiving Day parade. She would hover over my desk like one of those eastern fakirs who could levitate. Then she would slap the nearest desk with her yardstick, and like the good drill sergeant she was, bark out orders to pick up our pencils and start writing our numbers. We had not received orders to go forth and multiply; we had yet to add and subtract.

Other teachers would put up various warm and fuzzy scenes along the walls of their classrooms, which would change with the season. Miss Dahl's classroom was lined with useful things such as letters and numbers. If you wanted something warm and fuzzy you would just have to wait for the pictures in the Dick, Jane, and Sally reader. "Don't eat any of the paste," she told us. "It's made from horses' hooves."

Then there was the day one of the other teachers was admonishing one of his scholars for academic shortcomings. Miss Dahl reminded her counterpart that he must remember to be especially kind to slower students. Miss Dahl said it was almost certain the teachers would be working with them later on when they won a seat on the school board. When booksellers came to school, the principal would send them to Miss Dahl. If they made it back alive, Mr. Thompson knew they must have a good product. There wasn't much sugar in Stella Dahl.

I was never much of a student back then, but the last thing I wanted was to create any trouble with Miss Dahl. If I had been among the majority who did things with their right hand, or if left-handed scissors had been invented, things might have been better between us. But alas, I was a south-paw. I don't know who invented left-handed scissors, but I bet whoever it was had a teacher like Stella Dahl. Learning how to cut paper with my wrong hand was one of the major challenges of my life. At first I tried to turn the scissors upside down and use my left hand. Miss Dahl picked me up by my ear and lifted me out of my seat like a rag doll. "There isn't going to be any of that here, Michael Hillman. You're going to learn to cut the right way even if it takes until spring."

It got so I hated those scissors. They were short and stumpy with rounded ends so we couldn't hurt ourselves, or poke out the eyes of our classmates. I am convinced to this day that before the start of the school year, they sent the scissors in to be dulled on some machine. The scissors had been used by countless sweaty little fists by the time our year came, and I swear you couldn't cut butter with them on a warm summer day.

It wasn't that I didn't want to cut with my right hand. When Stella Dahl slapped my desk and told me to pick up my scissors and "cut," I would have cut anything. I remember looking out the window at a large white pine, thinking of it as a possible good-will offering or extra curricular project. I would have gladly offered to cut it down with my short, stumpy pair of wrong-handed scissors. I probably would have had about as good a chance cutting down the pine as I did cutting through the thick colored paper Miss Dahl gave us to practice on.

Many of the real triumphs that year were lost for me. Miss Dahl did not believe in excessive amounts of praise. Before we went on to second grade she made sure all of her students knew what they needed to know. We all worked hard for her. None of us wanted to be on the two-year plan. If you did something such as learning to read and write, you were doing your job. In her mind such things were not accomplishments that elicited praise.

The final memory I have of Miss Dahl came the following fall. I had made it out of first grade in one year and felt extremely fortunate. Then I lucked out and landed Ester Erickson as my second grade teacher. Ester Erickson was a sweetheart. I felt like Brer Rabbit safe at home in the briar patch.

One day I was looking out the window and saw someone running out the south doors of the school. It was my friend Richard. He was running as fast as he could. He was doing his best because only a short distance behind thundered Miss Dahl.

She looked like an avenging goddess out of a Wagnerian Opera. She was waving her yardstick over her head in her right hand like a scimitar. Her left hand was balled into a fist, which she was shaking in the general direction of the young truant who was making tracks towards home. *See Richard. See Richard Run. Run. Run. Run!* – (Feet don't fail him now!)

The last time I saw Miss Dahl was years later. I was home from college. When I stopped to visit with Mother, she informed me Miss Dahl was ill in the hospital. Mother was always trying to get me to do the right thing, and during the course of our visit, she suggested it would be a nice thing for me to go and visit my old first-grade teacher.

"What's the matter with her?" I asked.

"She's old, Michael. She's running out of steam, and I'm sure she'd love a visit from one of her students."

I was trying to think of a good reason why I was too busy to go and see her. "She never liked me, Mother. She yelled at me, and pulled my ears. I still can't bring myself to cut paper in public."

Mother gave me one of her is-this-the-best-you-can-do *looks*. "I've done the same thing to you myself when you needed it," she said, "and you still come and see me. Miss Dahl taught you to read and write. I think you owe her a visit."

I couldn't win, and I knew it.

Later that day I walked up to the nurses' station at the hospital. "Which room is Miss Dahl in?" I asked.

The nurse looked up at me and told me Miss Dahl was in Room 22. The lights were off in Room 22. At first I thought I had lucked out and she would be asleep. I felt like Thesesus entering the lair of the Minotaur. It took my eyes a little time to adjust to the dim light. When I looked down on the bed I saw a small figure rolled up in a loose fetal position. At first I thought I entered the wrong room. The illusion of childhood memory was giving way to the reality of the present. Miss Dahl looked deflated. She no longer seemed big and foreboding. She looked small and fragile.

I cleared my throat. The form on the bed turned and

rolled over. "Miss Dahl," I said, "you probably don't remember me."

It was all I got a chance to say. A very familiar voice stopped me cold. "Shut up! You probably still can't cut with scissors, Michael Hillman."

I was stunned. "You really do remember me, Miss Dahl?"

"I remember all my children, Michael Hillman, even left-handed ones like you. Thank you for coming, but if you don't mind, I want to take a nap."

Then she rolled over and went back to sleep. Not knowing what else to do, I walked out of the room. It was the last time I ever saw Miss Dahl.

I'm glad mother talked me into making that visit to Miss Dahl. Mother was right. Stella Dahl deserved at least that much. At times I have looked back on that last visit, and felt I should have said something else. I should have said thank you for teaching me to read and write, and to add and subtract. That thanks to you I went on and started to write stories. But that would have been a little too much sugar for Miss Dahl.

In second grade I found my Miss Ida. Her name was Ester Erickson. She was like the grandmother I never had. Ester Erickson never raised her voice, kept a handkerchief in her sleeve, and smelled of lavender. I can't remember a thing she taught me. All I remember was she was nice; as sweet as northern sugar ever got.

In first grade I met the best and only drill sergeant I ever needed, who taught me what I could do, and reminded me what I couldn't. Sometimes that's all the sugar we need.